SHIPS

THAT HAVE MADE HISTORY

By GREGORY ROBINSON

ILLUSTRATED WITH PAINTINGS
& DRAWINGS BY THE AUTHOR

HALCYON HOUSE : NEW YORK

HALCYON HOUSE *editions are published and
distributed by Blue Ribbon Books, Inc.,
386 Fourth Avenue, New York City*

PRINTED AND BOUND BY THE CORNWALL PRESS, INC., FOR
BLUE RIBBON BOOKS, INC., 386 FOURTH AVE., NEW YORK CITY
Printed in the United States of America

THE ENDEAVOUR, 1768

TABLE OF CONTENTS

GREGORY ROBINSON

FEW men are better fitted to give expression to the ships of the past than Gregory Robinson. Although authentic records of many of these vessels long have been available, the artists of past generations who depicted the ships of their time made but little use of them and were, for the most part, not seamen and knew little about the sea. Therefore the pictures which have come down to us of these early craft are unconvincing to the seaman or to those who know ships. While, perhaps, good examples of the art of the period, we are quite certain that they would not have satisfied the men who sailed in those ships. Drawings were usually out of proportion, details of hull and rigging were inaccurate, and the ships and sea as they show them do not fill the eye of a seaman. Yet until now these old paintings were all that we had on the vanished fleets of the thirteenth to the nineteenth century.

Gregory Robinson not only has the seaman's eye and instinct, but he has also dug deeply into the archives to get essential facts of the ships about which he writes and paints. He is one of the original members of the Society of Nautical Research and a frequent contributor to the Journal of that Society. He has sailed around the world on a square-rigged ship, and he has had access to the drawings in the Admiralty and the records in the British Museum. Material that he has uncovered from many available sources has enabled him to present with his brush convincing ships of the past, and particularly of those ships that have played an important part in the spread of the Anglo-Saxon race.

Nor are the sturdy men who sailed in these ships any the less convincing than the ships themselves. For, stripped of the glamour and romance with which history too often clothes the great figures of the past, Gregory Robinson shows us these seamen and leaders as in all likelihood they were in the flesh. Sailors to the core, bold, adventurous, they were nevertheless human beings, swayed by the same emotions and motivated by the same instincts as other seamen of their time. In writing of them as he does you are shown the men as they lived, and as they met the day-by-day problems of their long and arduous voyages. For instance Drake, the great freebooter, had no illusions as to the character of his voyage and cannily made sure that Queen Elizabeth, his patroness, was still on the throne before entering port on his return, lest otherwise he might have much explaining to do to save his skin. And Christopher Columbus, formerly a wine salesman, was a past master at driving a bargain for his services on his first voyage; nor did he scruple to let the poor seaman who first sighted land in the New World get beaten out of the prize offered for that eagerly awaited moment of the voyage. Human they were, but big as well; and as drawn by Mr. Robinson's pen they satisfy the conception of the sailor of today as to what the sailors of the past were like.

The author has here presented his whole subject, both drawings and text, in the way most likely to interest not only the yachtsman but also the layman who wants facts and not images of the fancy.

HERBERT L. STONE.

I

A FOURTEENTH CENTURY SHIP

A FOURTEENTH CENTURY SHIP, CIRCA 1300

A FOURTEENTH CENTURY SHIP

Careful Research Gives Us a Good Idea of Its Form, Construction and Accommodations

BEFORE considering the ships in which our forefathers sailed the wet seas 'round, it seems to me that it would be well to make quite sure that in our own minds there are no wrong ideas. And, first, it would be well to realize that although science and education have quickened us so that we move more briskly than our forefathers, yet our pace of mind is not altogether beyond comparison with that of their hesitating steps. We still walk warily and inherit something of the paternal gait.

Future ages will wonder at our slow methods of construction, for, likely as not, our descendants will run their ships all hot into a mould, merely leaving them to cool before launching. They will wonder why we held so long to a hull form which was helpful for sail but a hindrance to power-driven craft; they will wonder why it was so long before we thought of streamlining our hulls above water; they will wonder why we clung to a dozen useless things, the uselessness of which our dull wits have not yet realized. There will be wonderment again at the time-lag in our sea language — why, after two hundred years of wheel usage we still paid respect to the tiller, and why it took an international conference on helm orders to make some of us recognize the existence of that wheel. They will be sorely puzzled when they read that liners still *sailed* from New York long after they had been provided with engines of enormous horsepower, sailing on in spite of gasoline and the all-electric engine. Yes, we have outpaced the language, certainly; we take quicker steps than the Old Man, but we are still a long long way from the last word in shipbuilding.

We may be sure that when our efforts in naval architecture come to be considered years hence, our successors will say, "Wonderful!" in the same tone of voice as we do when we gaze at the pictures of the queer old arks of yesterday. They will be less captious if they know something of our difficulties, as our criticism will be the kindlier for knowledge of the Old Man's troubles. The troubles of those who have dealings with the sea start early, so perhaps you will forgive me if I begin at the beginning and tell that part of the tale which has been told before.

When, in the early dawning, man wandered from home and came to the waterside, he began to think how he might use the sea. He observed the form of the fish and set about to imitate it, using the handiest material. First, he made a frame with backbone and ribs; to it he bound reeds, lashing the ends together; then he pitched it within and without so that you could not see the wood for the caulking. As his hand caught up a little on his head, planks were substituted for reeds, the caulkers drew less wages than the carpenters, and the ship moved into deeper waters. She was of light scantling and smooth sided — carvel-built, as we say — and could be easily paddled with the hand, and this man who went south, faced forward as he went. Now the man who went north was hardier and probably had less mental capacity. He came to a river, and, according to the poets, saw on the other side a lady whom he loved. So, sitting astride a convenient fallen tree, he with his feet propelled himself across. Before the return journey, wishing to keep his bride out of the wet, he burned a hollow in the tree and put the lady in it. Time passed; he went voyaging again, and to keep the children from falling out he pegged a cloven board one strake high to his dugout. At two strakes high, he needed support inside to hold them up, and found grown knees in the oaks around him for that purpose. This ship was of heavy scantling necessitating all his strength for her propulsion — paddling would not do. He invented the thole pin and the oar, brought his legs in to help the arms, and put his broad back into the work.

Now, you may not believe these two stories. I confess that I am not too sure about the first, though the second seems likely; there is a woman in it, and there is a woman in all true stories. Besides, when occasionally a primitive dugout is uncovered, washboards are found raised on the more solid structure and there can be little doubt of the course of development in the case of the northern boat. Slowly, she became more clench than dugout, as old man north became more skillful as carpenter than as gardener, until only garboards and keel were carved in one. And, finally, the reader will observe his completely clench-built dinghy a-stern, and remember that when she was building in the yard they put the planking to the keel and stem and sternpost, adding the frame as if it were an afterthought, whereas he will call to mind that when his carvel-built yacht was building, the frame came first and the planking was bolted to it, as in the ship of the man who went south.

We know that when ships begin to emerge from the prehistoric darkness into the dim twilight of the Middle Ages we find the two types marked — in the Mediterranean all vessels, great and small, carvel-built; while in the north even the great ships in which the Kings of England and France fought, in the fourteenth century, were clench-built. And to this day the characteristic of the smallest fishing boat up the Straits is her smooth side, while small carvel-built boats appear only fitfully in the north.

Yes, perhaps there is something in those two stories.

In the vessels in which man pulled, as distinguished from those which he paddled, the planks upon which he sat were constructional as well as convenient parts of the ship. Before the invention of the rudder on the middle line of the ship, when one steered with a board on the starboard side, it was necessary to have a rigid fulcrum. This was given by a large beam across the quarters with the ends projecting outboard. In the south this beam was called the *hameron*. At the bluff of the bow was a similar beam laid across the upper works, called a *catena*, whose ends were used for catting the anchor. (Surely, it was a punning fellow who later painted cats' heads upon the ends.) Theword *hameron* seems to have some connection with hook, and *catena* is a chain, which indicates their common structural purpose of holding the spreading bows and quarters. When man came to make sail it was necessary to give the mast direct support as high up as possible; therefore, a mast beam was laid across her upper works, tying them in and giving security to the shrouds. In the sailing vessel proper it would seem that this mast beam was laid over the main beam which had previously taken on the duty of tying in her breadth when the thwarts had been knocked away, and these two, with the hooks fore and aft, were fundamental parts of the frame.

Unfortunately, the evidence of early shipbuilding is largely pictorial, and since artists in all ages have taken full advantage of that license always granted to them by a kindly world, their testimony is none too reliable unless confirmed from other sources. But it would appear that, while in the northern vessels the main structural tie beams came outboard to serve another purpose, in the southern type all beams came through the planking to serve their own ends. Here is indication of an important difference in the method of building. Seemingly, in the latter case, the beam found first security in the great outer stringer, or wale, to which it was bolted; it was then bolted sideways to the timber head in passing and bolted down again to the inner stringer, with a stout covering board over to lock all. In the northern ships we know that the beam ends rested in the *clamp* (which was a range of thick stuff in the internal planking, or ceiling, as it was called) and was secured to the frame by side knees. The southern way was lighter and neater, but it had one serious defect in the difficulty of making the vessel watertight where the beams came through the outside planking.

It is obvious that with beams resting on the sheering wale any deck laid on them would have to follow that sheer — well enough when it was easy, but most inconvenient when it was quick. However, in early small craft decks were so laid and folk had to put up with it. But a visible external row of beam ends did not necessarily indicate a deck inside, for we know that later all great ships had a tier of beams in the hold upon which no deck was laid; and, therefore, in the case of the big carracks, we are not much wiser as to the lay of the decks by a view of the pictures. We may be sure, however, that in any ship which carried passengers the decks did not conform to the sheer throughout, and it seems possible that the framing of ancient accommodation decks in early Mediterranean craft consisted of longitudinal timbers, the carlings, towards the middle line, with internal shelf pieces at the sides, the light planking being laid 'thwartships instead of 'long-ships.

With the Norseman it was different. The southerners had already piled deck over deck before he had worried about a cover. When he did decide to lay his decks, he settled them where convenient, without any reference to the sheer, and with no indication to the outside world as to where he had placed them; but there is little doubt that they were laid dead level, parallel to the keel.

When the trade of the Mediterranean, overflowing through the Straits, spread itself into the main ocean and English and Baltic ships began to go south for purchase, shipwrights' secrets became common knowledge, and there was cross breeding between the descendants of dugout and built-up ships, of oar propelled vessels, and designed sailing ships. In size, the southern craft had far outstripped the northern; the galleys were of greater length, and the sailing vessels were of far greater carrying capacity. As to design, in the north was a boat with superstructure; in the south was a designed vessel with many decks, grown up, complete. In workmanship, there was no comparison; the south showed diagonal trussing and many other refinements which the north did not understand for centuries.

But the Mediterranean types were conceived when seafaring meant quick passages in fair weather from port to port. When the ocean test came they failed and faded away, and the ultimate universal type of sailing ship inherited more from the sturdy, rough-hewn Norseman. One early result of the traffic in ideas was the disappearance of the carrack's beam ends inboard and the adoption of the more seaworthy practice for their security. With a universal demand for grown knees came a fear of shortage, which continued, leading eventually to the invention of the iron knee. Then came the iron frame of the composite-built, and at long last the all-metal ship of today — step by step, and slow at that!

We do not know definitely when details were exchanged, how late or how soon, nor how much or how little went to the making of ships of the transitional period, so that it is not surprising that the replicas, models, and pictures of the *Santa*

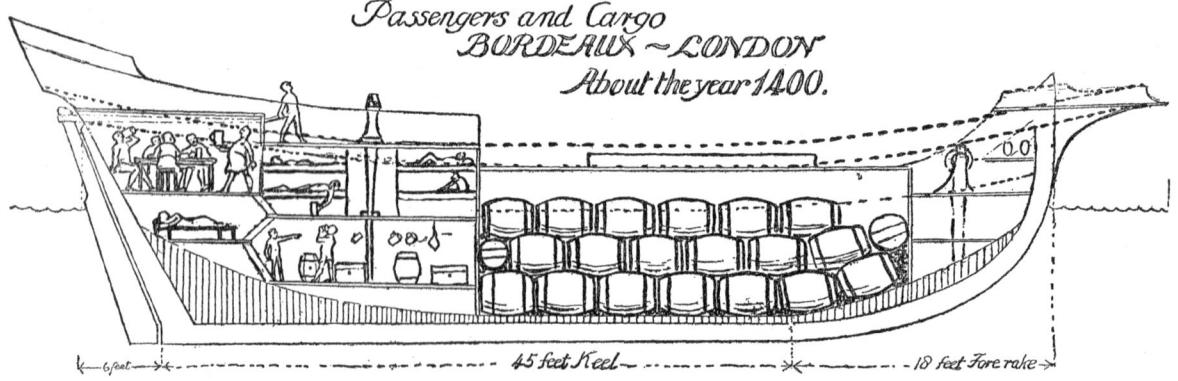

Passengers and Cargo
BORDEAUX ~ LONDON
About the year 1400.

6 feet — 45 feet Keel — 18 feet Fore rake

Maria made for our enlightenment differ materially. It is a wise archeologist who knows how much of either parent was in her. And there is another barrier to the gaining of exact knowledge of the ships of the early navigators and settlers. It is likely that future ages will find enough in the records to enable them to reconstruct a *Leviathan* or a *Mauretania*, but how little will they find of the little freighters of today! We are well on the road to discovery as to how the *Great Harry* was built, for there are records, but of the little tramps which carried the trade in the fourteenth, fifteenth and sixteenth centuries no records exist, and from this latter class the adventurers selected their ships and fitted them out as far as funds would permit. The *Mayflower* was but a hireling and carried vinegar, hats, hops and good red herring when she was not carrying Pilgrim Fathers, and the *Susan Constant*, which brought brave Captain John Smith to Virginia, mayhap later was taking woolen goods to Malaga, and loading Spanish wines, nuts and oranges home for London town. Of their outside appearance we know something. Aloft, we can rig them with fair accuracy; alow, we still find ourselves guessing. But there is no reason why we should not go below and have a look 'round in the dim light.

The old builder shared one difficulty with the yacht designer of today; he had to get much into little on a very short keel. True, the Old Man's clients did not expect a great deal of comfort, but they expected standing room, with a plank to lie upon and keep warm for the watch on deck. As the middle of his ship was filled with goods, he had to find accommodation in the ends, and as he believed in a fine run, deadwood and rising lines forced the ground floor high up in the structure before it could be made a platform of any reasonable area; as he came forward a little, he was able to come down a step or two, along again, then a step down into the hold where he was down on his floor timbers. With a step or two up again he was able to lay a platform over his fore peak. That was his ground tier, and that controlled the range of his decks above, fore and aft. It gave that old-shoe-like appearance to his ship which excites risibility in the modern beholder; but according to the conditions and his lights, the old man did pretty well with his space on the short keel length.

Before the shipwright felt sure of his scarphs, and until the keelson had grown up, he was limited in keel length by the size of a single tree — it must have been with great trepidation that a scarph was first introduced into the very foundation of the ship. His way of gaining waterline length was by raking stem and sternpost, holding them with great grown knees. Then, when more accommodation was needed above, he put a long external knee to carry a fore stage (or head, as later it was called) and some smaller knees as brackets for an overhanging gallery aft. "Here," we can almost hear him saying, "is the limit to which a ship can go." He had already decided on the proper breadth — no narrower for her stability, no wider for her going; he had already said she could be built no higher with seaworthy stuff, and it was no good building with anything else, for the sea would not have it. There could be no more accommodation. But accommodation had to be found for soldiers and passengers who looked for comfort.

At this juncture the house-carpenter, or castlewright, as he was called, was introduced into the shipyard. Uncompromising square castles, one fore and another aft, of dead square timber were erected over the living, sweeping lines of the ship. That frosty morning the master shipwright turned away and spat. These early castles were figuratively and, in fact, lash-ups, and likely enough the ship rolled them out of her in the essay; later, the heels of the uprights were tenoned into the wales and covering boards, and bolted where they could find a hold — upsparrings they came to be called. Hence our spar decks. They are easily recognizable in the early drawings — straight external framework from the mainmast aft, visible until the close of the sixteenth century, when they became more or less reconciled to the general form and scantling of the ship, as increased size enabled her to bear the heavier stuff aloft. The process of spar deck building, followed by absorption, still goes on. In the newest liners the shipwright seems to have pretty well smothered the house builder, but in the power-driven yacht the castlewright has fairly and squarely sat on the poor old shipwright. The castle-

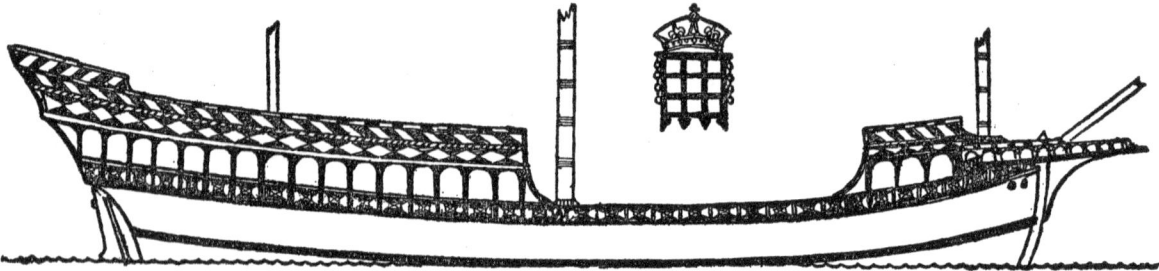

A SHIP of the latter end of the XV century before the sides were pierced for cannon. Below is the probable arrangement of decks and spar decks, while above may be seen the means taken by the shipwrights to hide up the disjointed work of the joiners and bring all into the sweeping lines and grace of the ship.

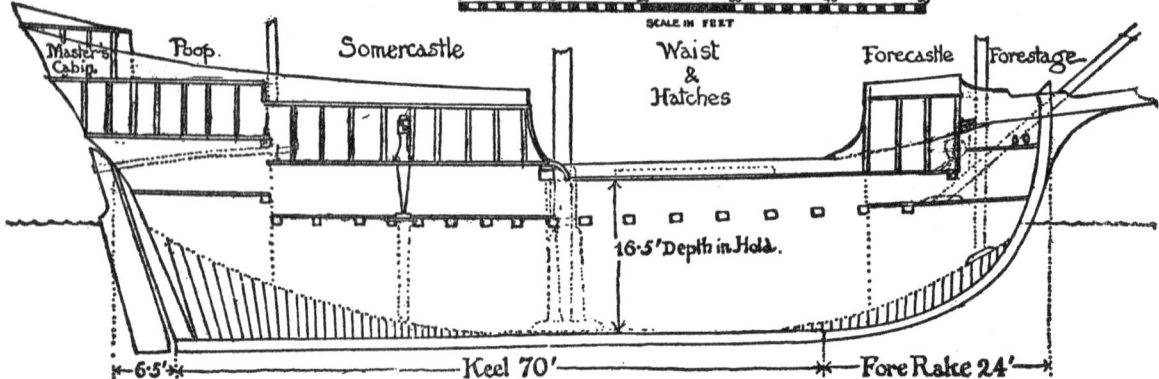

wright had, perforce, to take his levels from the ship's decks proper, and as they rose, so the spar decks rose.

At the top of the rise aft was one compartment which always had to crown all — the master's cabin, and by the beginning of the sixteenth century the master was indeed in a lofty position, for the ship proportionately was not unlike the city of New York, as lofty as it is long. I am judging in both cases by the pictures.

It was about this time that cannon were introduced in quantity and, to accommodate them, they proceeded to cut square holes along the broadside of the ship proper. Doubtless the shipwright warned them what would happen if they broke the girder strength of his sides with gun ports, saying, in his picturesque way "that the ship would sway in her back." She did. To repair this disaster the decks were made flush, giving a new longitudinal girder, tying in her ends. Of course it was not done all at once. First they removed any fall or cutting off by the mainmast, calling her *galleon-built*, for so went the galleon's decks; then they flushed her decks forward, and finally brought them up level aft, calling her *frigate-built*, for so lay the decks of the swift little ships which ran home with the treasure of the King of Spain. These steps were taken more rapidly than usual because structural and tactical needs were in harmony. The day of hand to hand fighting in wooden castles was dying, and it was realized that in future the day would be decided by the big gun, and the ship had best be constructed as one long battery. The flush-decked ship lasted out the wooden era; it was so that they designed the *Victory*, and so floats still the *Constitution* as a beautiful example of the shipwright's art.

To trace the development of sail in the square-rigged ship is comparatively simple. The single mast grew large, and when it had need to be of a girth which a single tree could not give, it would seem that a large oak foot was provided, in which the pine mast stood as a candle in a candlestick, and from the foot were raised great oak shores to support it; between the shores were fillings coaked and mortised together, the whole well woolded and tapered evenly upwards, so that the parrel of the main yard could descend gracefully. It was an imitation of the natural form of a lone straight tree growing thicker towards the ground, whereas the later type of made mast, which had a diameter less at the heel than at the partners, was composed of three or more pines, none of which went the whole length, and it was designed when the value of shrouds and stays was better appreciated.

It was a great affair, was the medieval mast, and when they hoisted the great yard with its halliards and truss-parrel, there were mighty yo-hoings and a long tally-on. Certainly, the sail was given plenty of flow and a good length of sheet, for our forefathers were great optimists, and ever hoped for a fair wind; but when hope was deferred, they could trim sail with braces, tacks, lifts, and the bowlines leading out to the bowsprit, so that it was not too inefficient in a peg to windward. In fair weather they laced a bonnet to the foot of the course (which is but our word *corpse* or *body*, disguised); to the foot of this, again, they laced a drabler for light airs. So they ghosted along. On their sails were painted strange devices — terrible beasts, queer birds, and quaint flowers, which, with their gaudy banners and league-long streamers, have given to us an impression of unreality. Under water, however, the shipwrights had given the ship a bold entry and a clean run, while on board was a crew of brown-necked hearty seamen who knew their business, and by and large the ship of the Middle Ages went very well.

By accident or design, the ship came by a foresail, the mast being stepped well in the eyes and finding good security in the catena. Very quickly, we may be sure, the mizzen followed, the mast finding a handy beam ready for its lashing. This mizzen sail was but half a sail, divided diagonally and more commonly known as a lateen. The learned believe the name derives from the fact that it was set in the middle line of the ship (*mezzo* meaning middle besides being mixed up with half). Anyway, it was the first fore and aft sail introduced into the square-rigged ship, coming from the south by way of the Portuguese coast. About the same time a spritsail appeared under the bowsprit — maybe after a dismasting when no other stick stood on which to spread a rag; or was it the *akateion* of the ancient Greek trireme, which was hoisted when she had had enough of battle under oars and would up stick and run — show the white feather?

When once the three masts were established, they took to themselves topsails; topgallants followed and were later crowned with royals. Sprit topmast, with its sail at bowsprit end, came and went. Staysails, jibs, and flying jibs, spankers, ringtails, and studding sails, with skysails over all, appeared, till everything was drawing, the braces clucking in the blocks like tightening fiddle strings, the following seas breaking and flattening under the forefoot of the full-rigged ship. So she came and passes.

II

THE SANTA MARIA

II
THE SANTA MARIA

THE SANTA MARIA, 1492

Genoa, general merchants, and, in particular, gold dust importers. (A member of the firm is said to have been responsible for the bright idea of the gold standard.) They were big people in the financial world and when prolonged wars had left money affairs in an unholy mess they were called in to assist the great Bank of St. George, whose head office was in Genoa, in straightening out matters. As a result, Europe was helped out of the fire into the frying pan. Columbus traveled in the Levant for the wine department, and later in sugar to Madeira, and by 1478 — when he married the well-to-do widow Perestrello — he had become a man of considerable business capacity. Together with an estate in the sunny little islands of Porto Santo, marriage brought him many charts, books and instruments which the late lamented had collected and left to his widow. Geography had been his hobby and he had money to indulge it.

The knowledge of these early connections, business and domestic, are as a spotlight on the interview between our hero and King Ferdinand and Queen Isabella. The romantic picture of the dreamy Italian sea captain in rags fades out and in its place we see clearly a confident commercial traveler with goods to sell. In effect, he said, "Twelve and one-half per cent to me of all the gold imported in the first voyage and you supply a ship. Ten per cent to me and my heirs forever of all the gold which may come from the lands I will discover of which I and my heirs will be Viceroys and Admirals — take it or leave it." Ferdinand of Spain, like King Joao of Portugal, thought the price too high, and without wasting any more words Columbus packed his bag for France.

The story goes on that a good priest approached Isabella and said, "Think of the poor heathen who might be converted," and Santangel, financial adviser to the Court, reminded Ferdinand that the port of Palos was in arrears with its taxes and could be ordered to supply the ship, so that there need be no initial outlay. It is not at all improbable that he reminded the King, too, that Lombardy bankers were charging 20 per cent on overdraft. So Columbus was asked to call again and on April 30th, 1492, the business was concluded. And what did Christopher Columbus know?

As a young man in the wine shops down in Sailor Town he had listened and drunk little while the seamen drank much and were loquacious. He had heard tales of men blown far out into the ocean; of the seas of the floating forest to the Canaries; he had heard the hard cases — the sceptics of the forecastle — laugh when they heard the tale retold; they had winked at him and said "seaweed." He had heard of strange flotsam which came ashore in the Azores from the westward. He might have suspected a westerly set branching off from the south-going current when he went voyaging to Guinea. He would have called to mind his old mother doing the family washing in the swirling stream, with the offscourings herding into the center of the swirls. He would have thought and reckoned that here might be a mighty ocean swirl with something out yonder to turn that westerly drift into an easterly current and account for the seaweed in the center — that which we now call the Sargasso Sea. Yes, it is often the application of some childish experience or simple observation which leads men on to great discoveries. Long residence in Madeira and Porto Santo had told him that the northeast trade wind followed the sun away south in winter, and betwixt the Azores and Madeira the wind hung more often westerly than easterly at that season.

Onlookers see most of the game, if they keep their eyes open, and Columbus, with his clear sharp eye and acquisitive mind, had collected much from the conversations of practical seamen. When, later, he acquired Perestrello's charts and books he was able to apply modern knowledge to ancient wisdom. Hippalus, the great Roman navigator, had in the first century noted the working of the trade winds in the Eastern seas; the Hindus had used them time out of mind, and we may be sure it was not by accident that the Canaries were chosen in preference to the Azores from whence to make a departure.

To help the good ships safe to port, he chose men who could be trusted to keep a sharp lookout, use the lead, watch the compass, and observe the pole star — seamen everyone — John de la Cosa, master and owner of the *Santa Maria*, and the brothers Martin and Vincent Pinzon, particularly Martin, captain of the *Pinta*, who led the little line of three ships into the New World.

It was sunrise on August 3rd, 1492, when the *Santa Maria, Pinta, Niña* slipped out of Palos and laid a course for the Canaries where they prepared themselves for the passage. On September 6th they left Gomera, but it was not until the 9th that they cleared the baffling calms of the islands and, through the tumbling, confused seas at the edge, came to the more regular swing of the trades. With what relief to them the Island of Ferro melted into the blue and purple and silver of the clouds on the eastern horizon those know best who have projected a long voyage, who have made a resolve and pursued it. We may be sure that Columbus, whose disappointments and vexations had been of long continuance, slept soundly the night he was shut of the land, and when in the morning watch he came on deck the sparkling fresh northeaster blew the cobwebs out of his mind and the gold dust out of his eyes as he stood Admiral of the Ocean.

Fair wind and fine weather, with the clouds marching steadily in good order from horizon to horizon by way of the arch, such was the order of the day and of every day. Porpoise, sheering close across the stem as though they would read the draft marked upon it and thereby better pilot the ship; birds over her wake as whippers in, seas hustling at her quarter, then passing swiftly ahead, leaving thin lines of foam as though they offered a tow — all seemed to entice, nothing to check the westward way. To those on board who knew the world was round came no fear, but to the others who pictured an edge and then Eternity there was dread

— for they had not all been too good, not all those men who signed on in Palos. So from sunrise to sundown they sailed on — gold in the morning, silver all day, gold in the evening, and at night the heavens were spangled with it.

When the trades blew fresh of nights and seas broke under their bows, the sound, they said, was as the sound of the trees when hard winds blew at home in Andalusia. As the darkness shut down, they always shortened sail for fear of running unawares upon one of those islands with which cartographers were wont to decorate their work. One such island we know appeared on a chart for no other reason than to give pleasure to the painter's wife. They were fortunate, however, in not having the anxiety of traffic, for the North Atlantic was a lonely place in 1492. We may imagine that the masters and their mates in the little flotilla had enough experience of seamen, in particular, and folk, in general, to know that work is the best cure for worry and the hands were kept pretty busy. Likely enough, had the masters' logs survived, we should have read — in Spanish, of course — of the "hands employed on various jobs, weather the same, winds northeasterly," day after day. Doubtless, too, the watch below slept soundly, turning out to grouse at their grub, and (under their breath) curse the boatswain when he turned them to. Sailors, they say, don't care; but, more surely, sailors don't change.

At last the winds came variable. The scent of burning wood now and again, land birds resting on yardarms, driftwood and other signs several times led to the reporting of Cape Flyaway.

At ten o'clock on the night of October 11th, Columbus thought he saw a light. At 2:00 a.m. on the 12th, just four hours afterwards, he saw a light beyond a doubt — the flash of the *Pinta's* gun as she sighted the land dead ahead. It was the prearranged signal. Roderick de Triana was the man who sang out from forward in the *Pinta*, and soon every man Jack in the ship saw it as plain as a pikestaff — breakers on a sandy beach capped with a row of dark trees. It was then that Martin Pinzon shattered the silence of the darkness and, slowly coming to the wind, waited for the others to come up. At daylight they anchored under the island which the Indians called Guanahani and which Columbus christened San Salvador.

For hundreds of years the identity of this spot was lost amongst the seven hundred odd cays and islands of the Bahamas; then, after much disputation, the opinion of Admiral J. B. Murdock, U. S. N., endorsed by the British Admiralty, was accepted and an Act of Parliament was passed granting to Watling Island the honor of the historic landfall. This was in 1926. The Act reaches back far. When Roderick de Triana came home in 1493, he put forward his claim to the 10,000 maravedis a year which had been promised to the man who first sighted land, only to find that the Admiral himself claimed it on the strength of the light which he maintained he saw in the night. The Admiral won. Unfortunately for Roderick, his good captain, Martin Pinzon, had died two days after reaching Palos — died of grief they said, but I do not believe it. Had he lived, it is sure he would have stood up for his own man; he would have asked Columbus why, believing he saw a light on land, he did not fire a cannon? Why he did not take a bearing and sail in upon it? He claimed to be a seaman; then why? That is about what he would have said. But Roderick de Triana, though he had it in his head, doubtless never got it beyond his throat; he came out purple and spluttering, shipped away for Barbary and there turned Turk. Now, by Act of Parliament, Roderick, rather late in the day, is proved right, for if you will look at the chart you will see that there is no land out to windward of Watling Island and all the islands in the Bahamas lie low. A native canoe? Commander R. T. Gould, R.N., pertinently asks what she was doing 35 miles off the nearest land and dead to windward? In any case, a canoe, with an Indian lighting his cigar, does not constitute a landfall. Perhaps, from off the land that night gold dust was blown into the eyes of the great Admiral. In the morning it was in all the eyes of all that company.

But it never blinded Columbus completely as it did some of those who displaced him soon afterwards. Thank heaven, we have not to tell their story here, for it is, indeed, an ugly one, the story of the little hell they made of Hispaniola. He came out to barter for gold and made no secret of it and, since he was working on a percentage basis, he wasted no time. The quest which began decently enough on October 12th developed eventually into that insane lust which gives the substance as it takes away the sense to enjoy. The Indians of Darien conceived the happy thought of putting gold at the ends of their arrows, hoping thereby to tempt the Spaniards to stoop and, thus catching them bending, slay them with the more ease. The story stands as a humorous savage comment on a civilization which has lost its humor.

The *Pinta* soon parted company and shortly afterwards the *Santa Maria* was wrecked and Columbus transferred himself to the *Niña*. Settling 38 people at Navidad, in Hispaniola, early in January, he set sail for home alone, but on the first day out he fell in with the *Pinta* again. Where Martin Pinzon had been and what he thought of it all we shall never know with certainty, for we have only what is written in the journal and the reported conversations of the Admiral. From these sources we gather that Martin Pinzon was ambitious. The passage was made largely in the latitude of the Azores, the track which afterwards became the recognized way home.

The magnificent reception Christopher Columbus received on his first return and the subsequent discredit and neglect need not be here recounted. He was a wise man and old, so that the discovery that kings and princes do not always stand by a contract surprised him less, perhaps, than the discovery of America.

Now a word about the ships. The *Santa Maria* was three-masted, having a fore and mainsail square, a mizzen, a maintopsail, and a spritsail set under the bow-sprit, and she is said to have been of 100 tons. These are the only facts we have to work upon. It is as well to be plain, for the production of two full-sized models, one of which has been reproduced in miniature again and again, has given an idea of certainty which the scanty evidence does not warrant. Although we do not know the order in force as to measurement in 1492 it would seem that the method used in Spain a hundred years later was: —

$$\frac{(\text{Length between perps:} \times \text{mean breadth} \times \text{depth in hold})}{80} - \frac{1}{20} = \text{burden,}$$

adding one-fifth for gross tonnage.

The contemporary English method ignored the length between perpendiculars. It was: —

$$\frac{\text{keel} \times \text{breadth} \times \text{depth in hold}}{100} = \text{burden, adding one-third for gross tonnage.}$$

The divisor varied between 90 and 100, but was generally nearer 100, and there were other small variations which need not be gone into at the moment. About this time a Spanish merchant ship which changed hands was found to be one-sixth less in English than her original gross tonnage, so that the *Santa Maria's* 100 Spanish tons, with her fifth added, would be 120 tons gross, while by English measurement she would be 100 tons gross and only 75 tons burden.

We have the dimensions of three English merchantmen of the period. Their average proportions of keel : breadth : depth is 4.26 : 2 : 1. Cargo carrying being a matter of pure economics, the proportions are likely to have been fairly constant the world over. As to the relation of keel length to l.b.p., a common proportion would be about 5 : 7, and a full breadth of 20 feet would be about 16 at the half height. With these figures in mind, let us see what can be done.

$$\frac{42 \times 20 \times 9}{100} = 75.6 + \frac{1}{3} = 100.8 \text{ tons gross.}$$

$$\frac{59 \times 16 \times 9}{80} - \frac{1}{20} = 100\frac{72}{80} \text{ *tonelada* or Spanish tons} + \frac{1}{5} = 121 \text{ *tonelada*.}$$

On this showing the *Santa Maria* might be: 59′ l.b.p., 42′ keel, 20′ beam, 16′ half breadth, 9′ depth in hold.

The *Pinta*, of 50 *tonelada* or 33 tons burden English: 47′ l.b.p., 30′ keel, 15.5′ beam, 11.5′ half beam, 7.5′ d.h.

The *Niña*, of 40 *tonelada* and 30 tons burden English: 46′ l.b.p., 30′ keel, 14′ beam, 11′ half beam, 7′ d.h.

The figures of the well-known *Santa Maria* reconstruction of 1892 were: 74′ l.b.p., 60′ keel, 25′ beam. They were based primarily on what was believed to be evidence of the size of the flagship's boat, but R. C. Anderson has shown that this evidence is non-existent. Secondly, reliance was placed on the ship's complement. It is known that altogether there were 87 people in the three ships and 40 is the number generally allotted to the *Santa Maria*.

The proportion in merchantmen of the period is believed to have been one man to every five tons, which would give a ship of 200 tons, but this evidence is disputed and speculative for it is reasonable to suppose that in the special circumstances of the voyage the ship would have had many supernumeraries. Certainly, in one hundred years there is likely to have been some modification in the method of calculating tonnage but it is unreasonable to accept an error of 100%.

Leaving the tonnage for the moment, let us turn to performances. Departure from Ferro to the landfall at Watling Island is 3,100 miles by the shortest route; therefore, the average speed was little more than 4 knots. But the best day's run is recorded as 200 miles, which means a speed of $8\frac{1}{2}$ knots. The highest speed of the replica of 1892, when she was pressed, was only $6\frac{1}{2}$ knots, rather pointing to an error in design. But there is one detail common both to the 1892 and the 1929 reconstructions which must have reduced the speed of these vessels considerably and that is the position of the external vertical timbers or upsparrings, the heels of which are brought so near the water that the slightest list would put them right in — a sad check to the way of the ship. The authority for the position of the heels is doubtless some pretty picture, but in dealing with practical affairs the rule should be: jettison the artists. The men who built the ships which made the memorable crossing had behind them the tradition of the Phœnicians and the Carthaginians, people who did big business in great waters; they knew that a ship must have an underbody as clean as a smelt or she would not go.

I do not think there are many speed records in the fifteenth century, but in 1525 four ships ran home from Porto Rico to St. Lucar Bar in 25 days. That is a distance of at least 3,600 miles, and they must have been ships with clean run. In 1575, Drake came from the Florida Channel to the Scilly Isles in 23 days in what is described as a small Spanish frigate. That is very good going. Of course, these passages are not comparable with *Dorade's* 17 and *Landfall's* 19 days by the longer route, but it does rather look as if, had Drake delayed his passage until 1926 and fallen in with *Jolie Brise* off the Bermudas, Martin (George, not Pinzon) might have found himself entertaining Master Francis Drake at breakfast any morning on the voyage home to Plymouth.

Unfortunately, we do not know the sail area of the *Santa Maria*, but we are not likely to be much out if we make the height of her topsail yard from the water line equal to her water line length, and her main yard a little more than twice her beam. The topsail was small and was probably not sheeted out to the yardarm; the sizes of the foresail, mizzen and spritsail can only be guessed. It seems that the *Pinta* was square-rigged, certainly on the foremast, before she left Palos, and that the *Niña* was converted at the Canaries, but details are scanty and the wise artist (for the present) will put both the smaller ships out of sight and the flagship hull down, for the arrangement of *Santa Maria's* upper works is none too sure.

The English ton measured 60 cubic feet, and originally two butts went to the tun of wine. In Spain the *tonelada de arqueo* measured only 53.44 cubic feet, so that the *Santa Maria*, in her ordinary trade, would have had 5,344 cubic feet of cargo space in which were stowed 200 casks, but I do not suppose she was filled up to her coamings when she went west and room would have been found in the hold for many of the crew. Nevertheless, it does not leave much accommodation in her ends, and it is probable that between main and mizzen, superstructure of about the scantling of a hen coop gave sleeping space for some of the extra people. If Columbus occupied what was usually John de la Cosa's berth, Master John made shift with a box about the size of a large kennel on the poop. I imagine that in none of this additional accommodation would there have been full headroom and that although it made a little extra windage it did not imperil her stability.

From these considerations, it would appear that what is required in a replica of the *Santa Maria* is an underbody which could be pushed up to a speed of about ten knots, could give 5,344 cubic feet of cargo space, and could accommodate 39 souls and a sea cook in considerable discomfort. No one, I hope, will endeavor to construct an expensive model on the figures I have given; I am sure they need correction by a committee consisting of a practical seaman, a naval architect, a shipowner, a stevedore and perhaps a schoolmaster. When they have come to some agreement, doubtless they will submit their plans to the Society for Nautical Research, the society which, beginning with a small band under Carr Laughton some twenty odd years ago, has since developed under Geoffrey Callender's secretaryship into an international body of naval archaeologists. We can then hope to get within an inch or two of the proud ship which carried brave Christopher Columbus across the Western Ocean.

III

THE SPANISH TREASURE FRIGATE

III

THE SPANISH TREASURE FRIGATE

THE SPANISH TREASURE FRIGATE, 1590

Indeed, so far as planning was concerned, things could hardly have been bettered. As early as 1508 Amerigo Vespuccio was appointed pilot-major and with his staff he trained and examined pilots, sending them to sea again for a year if they failed; certificates went with all navigational instruments used, while a standard chart was prepared under Amerigo's supervision. So came the word "America" on the map; though it would appear that it was a toss up as to whether they would not write Jerrisabellica — America was born lucky. A board was responsible for the surveying of all ships intended for the West, and they were inspected light, loaded, with a final look around at the farewell buoy to insure against overloading and to make sure that they went armed against an enemy. All of which sounds modern enough. Everybody was registered and examined as to financial position and morals, care being taken to see that no blasphemers crossed. But officials were bribed, blasphemy soon broke out in America, unregistered goods were shipped in the night, and regulations were not carried out. Rogues and fools did their best to wreck the machinery. And all of this has a modern sound, too.

The sailing orders were explicit. From San Lucar Bar they ran for the Canaries. After completing with wood and water, they made a departure from Ferro; the course was S for twenty-four hours and then away W by S across the ocean for the Island Deseada. Here, if the fleets for the Spanish Main and Mexico had sailed together, they parted; the former had an easy navigation, laying a course for Cape de la Vela and so comfortably along to Nombre de Dios or Porto Bello. The Mexican fleet passed through Galleons Channel, which is betwixt Antigua and Guadaloupe, by Santa Cruz, Cape Roxo, Mona, and Saona, into the Bay of Neyba in San Domingo, for refreshment. Then S to Alta Vela, WNW for Cape Tiburon, passing north of Nevasa to Cape Cruz in Cuba, and across the bay of Jardin de la Reigna (which queen's garden is a rockery) to sight the Island of Pines. After passing Cape Corrientes and San Antonio, it was a bold NW into the Gulf, then W for a landfall well to the north of their port — that was, in winter. In summer time they chanced their arm, wending their way through the shoals of Yucatan, so at last into San Juan de Uloa. For the masters of the clumsier old wagons this last passage must have been a nightmare. If the Nombre de Dios fleet had sailed from Spain alone, a more southerly course was made, bringing them to Galleons Passage, between Tobago and Trinidad. Thus they came to fetch it away, sometimes alone and sometimes together, but once the treasure was aboard, then, they always made the ocean passage as one fleet.

Havana was the rendezvous. In summer time the great convoy was swept out through the Florida Channel up north of the Bermudas to 39°. Then, huddled together, and of necessity at the pace of the laggards, they crawled down their easting, making the Island of Corvo in the Azores. In winter, they left Bermuda to the north and in 37° made for the Island of Santa Maria. From the Azores by way of Cape St. Vincent, thence, if they were favored, home to San Lucar Bar.

As early as 1520 the game of hanging about on the horizon and pouncing upon the stragglers was being played, first by French privateers and very soon afterwards by a swarm of English, Dutch, and Flemings, plain or mixed. They hung thickest around the Azores for here was an added chance of an East Indian carrack if they were men enough to tackle her, besides the convenience of being able to fill up barricoes with water and hang on a week or two longer, hoping. Some of them went missing, many came home more than half starved, but enough made large fortunes to advertise the business and keep up the numbers.

Those who have had to do with convoy work will best appreciate the difficulties and weariness of it in the days of sail. The shepherding of a crowd of vessels under steam has its anxieties, but the differences between units is mainly confined to speed forward; in sail was added the rate of speed sideways, for some of them were leewardly old haystacks and the wonder is that they kept together at all. In modern times the periscope is close work and sudden death; in the old days, evilly disposed topsails peeped over the horizon at you and kept on peeping, keeping up the anxiety for weeks. Doubtless, the Admiral of the Flota, as the senior officer of the West Indian convoy was called, went white at forty. But somewhere about 1589 he was relieved of a great responsibility when it was arranged that the more valuable cargoes should cross independent of the fleet.

For many years those splendid fellows, the Biscay fishermen, had been working the Newfoundland Banks in flush-decked vessels, bringing home dried fish for the Friday dinners of good Catholics. With very little alteration in design the smelly fish carrier was converted into a carrier of gold ingots and silver bar. The design probably owed something, too, to the little ships which had been carrying the treasure from the Main to Havana for some years and it was in the latter place that they were built. From *Biscainers* they came to be called *galley zabras, pataches* and other funny names, and, eventually, *frigates*. We may be sure they kept their fishing crews, but these had to put up with a guard of southern Spaniards housed on deck aft. Sick, cold and sorrowful those soldiers must have been as these proper ocean racers came lashing across the North Atlantic in winter. Figuratively, and in fact, the smartest men-of-war never saw the way they went.

It was some years after their first launching that England was trying to find out what they looked like, and from a spy at Havana came a picture of a dreadful looking box; the drawing is still preserved in the Record Office. Perhaps it was a case of counter-espionage, perhaps the poor fellow could not draw, but, certain it is, the result is a gross libel on those fine little ships. Some day, maybe, their lines may be discovered in Spain and we shall know what they were like. From particulars gathered here and there, they would seem to have been of about 200 tons, much longer in the keel, and of less beam than the orthodox ships of the period. I have no experience of it, but I imagine gold would be good stuff for ballast lying snug by the keelson. It was a hint to the Spanish designer, which he took, and, clapping on more sail, he produced a flyer. There is no record of any of these early birds being caught with treasure on board. This is not the end of the story of the frigate, which may as well be briefly related here.

When war ceased with Spain, they made a nest for themselves at Dunkirk from whence they terrorized the English Channel, often holding up the coal trade in the North Sea so that prices in London went skyrocketing and poor folk went with cold feet. They were manned by all sorts, including English and Scotsmen. The English shipwrights produced the ten *Lion's Whelps* to catch the Dunkirkers; the Dunkirkers sailed two feet to their one and snapped up merchantmen under their noses.

In early days the Earl of Warwick bought a Dunkirker and used her privateering, but it was not until 1635 that the Navy, having caught a little frigate called *Nicodemus*, decided to copy her, she having the reputation of running away from everything "as a greyhound does from a little dog." So the following year were launched the *Roebuck* and the *Greyhound;* they seem still to have been on the beamy side and of only about 100 tons. The latter ended her career twenty years later in a sheet of flame and glory. After being overwhelmed by two privateers and having one hundred of the enemy in her, Captain George Wager put a light to his magazine. But long before that, English designers had produced a whole string of fine frigates, faster and harder hitters than anything that came out of Dunkirk, and in Cromwell's day, such ships as *Adventure, Nonsuch, Constant Warwick, Tiger, Dragon* and *Sapphire* cleaned up the Narrow Seas. It is Peter Pett of Ratcliffe who has the distinction of building the first British frigate.

By the eighteenth century, what with unintelligent copying, and overloading with ordnance — that eternal error in ship design of trying to put a quart into a pint pot — the frigate had become a slug. The renaissance came from France towards the end of the century when she built many fine, graceful vessels. Unfortunately for her, one of the best fell into British hands soon after launching and supplied a much needed pattern — her name was *Revolutionaire;* she revolutionized frigate design in England.

How much or how little the *Constitution* was influenced by these later developments I do not know — there would have been by that time an American tradition. But when you next go to view *Old Ironsides,* raise your hat to the memory of old Mr. Peter Pett of Ratcliffe who gave her hitting power without impairing her speed. You will find gold dust and silver ships in her bilges and you will smell fish all over her. And maybe when you go racing to Santander you will find yourself shaking hands with the descendants of the man who gave her that essential quality of all good ships — seaworthiness.

IV

THE GOLDEN HIND

THE GOLDEN HIND, 1577

THE GOLDEN HIND

The First Englishman to Sail Around the World Stood a Chance of Being Hanged As a Pirate—Instead He Was Knighted

IN THE autumn of 1580, a league or so southwest of Plymouth, some fishermen were hailed by a ship which they had been watching for some time. As she came slowly to the wind she revealed herself as a seaworn yet seaworthy vessel. Her sails were a patchwork of varying shades of mouse gray, the tar was out of the bolt ropes and there was a bleached look about her braces and bowlines; her upper works hinted that they had once been green and white, and as though not wishing to disturb the quiet scheme, she was flying no colors.

To the fishermen she seemed somehow familiar, and any doubts they may have had as to her nationality were put to rest when, in an unmistakable Devon accent, they were asked whether Queen Elizabeth still lived. The question answered, there came from the poop of the ship a cheery, "A good haul to you, my masters," and as she filled and bore away for Plymouth she showed to the men in the small boat a golden hind on her escutcheon. Their sharp eyes saw that quickly enough, but their more slowly working minds were some little while in realizing that there had once been a pelican painted where was now a golden hind, and that the man who had wished good luck to their fishing, was the man for whom half the world was looking — Master Francis Drake.

It was not altogether surprising that the realization was slow. The picture which had been in men's minds for many a day hardly seemed to fit the gray little ship and the weather-beaten man who had looked over the side. Wild tales of fabulous loot had been current throughout the country, and in all the taverns of the western seaports Drake and his doings had caused much barrel-thumping and banging of pots. Some seamen knew that there were good times in Spain if religion were kept out of conversation; they had happy memories of dark eyes and tresses, of sunshine and good red wine, and now they felt that the last farewells had been said to the ladies of Spain. To others, who had not found favor in the eyes of the dear Spanish ladies, or who were hot-gospellers and banged their Bibles with much force — as other men banged their pots — Drake was the man. As it was among the seamen, so it was among the merchants in the city; the elders were shocked and frightened, for Spain had been a good customer for many years, and with the news, came the certainty that their trade must soon cease. It was to the younger merchants, who had all to make and none to lose, that the news of Drake's exploits was welcome. At the court, while some looked gay, others looked grave — the innermost circle round the throne turned not all one way. And how stood the center of all, Elizabeth, by the Grace of God Queen of England?

The leading actor in the great sea drama, of whom we have caught a glimpse as he passed onto the stage for the last act, knew perfectly well how the dear lady stood, and knew how things were likely to turn so long as she reigned Queen of England. His question to the simple fishermen as to the health of his Sovereign Lady has been quoted by a modern historian as showing the deep place Elizabeth occupied in the hearts of her people, and we may suppose in the heart of Francis Drake in particular. It may be so, but this is certain, that had the answer been that the Queen was dead, the *Golden Hind* would not have gone into Plymouth, and while eventually her captain might have gone into mourning, he would first have found a quieter and more remote haven wherein to deposit his cargo. He said as much as this himself — remarkably frank by nature was Francis Drake.

As the *Golden Hind* disappeared round Rame Head those fishermen minded how that same ship had left Plymouth three years before — yes, she was called the *Pelican* then — bound for Alexandria with a general cargo, and purposing to bring home a cargo of currants, it was said. But they had not believed much in that story, for it was not the sort of trade her captain had much experience in; and when a year afterwards the *Elizabeth*, one of the ships that sailed with her, returned home to say that she had seen the *Pelican* in the neighborhood of Magellan Straits and feared that she was lost, Plymouth folk were sorry for Captain Drake, but not surprised to hear that the currants were still waiting on the quay at Alexandria. After an interval, came another yarn that the captain had been caught and hanged by the Spaniards; then it turned out that someone said that they would hang him if they could catch him — and Devon folk reckoned they wouldn't, ever.

A week or so after the ship's arrival, country bodies along the West road saw a stout, short, bearded man riding a horse towards London, awkward, perhaps, in the saddle, but firm enough, and he rode in company with his men, any one of whom might have been taken for that shipman who, with Chaucer, had made a pilgrimage to Canterbury two hundred years before — "the hot summer had made their hue all brown." But they had been a deal nearer the sun than that older salt of Dartmouth, and their present journey was hardly a pilgrimage; they were, in fact, in attendance on their master who was on his way to the city to meet the shareholders of the little company of which he was managing director, at which happy meeting he was about to declare a dividend of 4700 per cent.

The principal shareholder was Elizabeth Tudor, and that gracious lady was right glad to see him. For six hours she sat closeted with her blue eyed sailor. He, wise fellow, had brought with him little sample packets of gold and pearls and emeralds, and little rolls of gay fal-lals to brighten any dull passages in his tale.

Meanwhile, Bernardino de Mendoza, Ambassador of his Most Sacred Majesty Philip, King of Spain and the Indies to the court of St. James, cursed and cursed and cursed in the cold outside.

Of the beginning of that memorable voyage there was little that could have interested the Queen, and most of it she had heard a year previously from Captain Winter when he came home in the *Elizabeth*. It was a record which differed little from the voyages of the period — when men took what they might require where they might find, and trusted to luck whether it were called piracy or not. There was the usual run of the weather, the brisk northeast trade winds succeeded by the calms of the tropics, the beautiful sunshine of the southeast trades making by contrast more dreary and dreadful the rains and squalls of the southern latitudes. There was too little fresh water for drink, and a deal too much salt for comfort, intervals of sunshine hardly long enough to dry soaking shirts and sodden bedding, sickness and cursings and rotten food — no story this to set before a queen.

There was the story of the man who knew too much, with its terrible ending which belonged to this part of the voyage. This the Queen cut short at its first telling, and in polite circles it has not been told since.

As the *Golden Hind*, the *Elizabeth* and the *Marigold* cleared Magellan Straits and burst through into the South Seas, they were met by a great storm during which the *Marigold* foundered with all hands. The *Elizabeth*, losing company, lost hope and returned home to England. The *Golden Hind* held on through bitter cold and blinding sea smoke. Driven far to the southward, after two weary months, Drake was able to bring her north again clear of the giant rollers into pleasant weather and at last to close the land.

Not a whisper of Drake's coming had reached the sunlit shores of South America. For thirty years no soul had succeeded in the Magellan passage, and Spain in her pride felt that where she had failed there was no hope of success for others. She had beaten most of the life out of the natives of the country, and while on the coastline there were fitful troubles to deal with, on the sea itself there was no danger and all ships went unarmed. So it was that in December, 1578, the *Captain of Morial*, a fine ship, lay snugly at anchor in Valparaiso Harbor with most of the crew ashore. Sighting a ship coming in from seaward, those remaining on board made preparations to entertain the newcomers with a jar of wine, and as the vessel entered they saluted her with a roll of the drum. The stranger came on and fell alongside, and the next moment the hospitable Spaniards found themselves driven below hatches. Having made all secure, Drake landed to collect a fair supply of fresh provisions and wine, a chalice and an altar cloth from the chapel; then, returning to the ship, he released his prisoners, save John the Greek whom he kept for a pilot, and towed his prize away. Rifling her as they went, she produced £80,000 in gold and a great cross set with emeralds. It was a bright beginning.

At Coquimbo, landing for water, the Spaniards were found in force, and Drake lost a man whom he could ill spare — it was a warning that he had better not meddle too much with the land. The new pilot brought them to a quiet haven where, unmolested, the Englishmen were able to put together a small pinnace. Having now abandoned hope of her consort, the *Golden Hind* stood away north early in the new year.

Drake, in the pinnace close inshore, searched the bays, while his ship sailed a league to seaward — so they worked their way up the coast. At Pisagua some of the crew, stretching their legs ashore, found a Spaniard sleeping on the beach with 4000 ducats in silver bar beside him; the silver went into the boat, the gentleman they left to his siesta. Another was met jogging along quietly with eight well-loaded llamas, they lightened the load by eight hundredweight of silver. This was very well, but Drake, who years before had climbed that tree in Panama, had seen the vision of a Sea of Gold and this seemed to him a sea of small silver. They must hasten on, too, for he knew that ashore the horses were struggling through the mountain passes to give warning to the settlements further north that pirates had broken into the South Sea.

So, under the mighty sunbaked cliffs of the Atacama Desert, the Devon men were sweating at the sweeps in the hot windless mornings, praying that the breeze would come good and hearty from the southward in the afternoon and waft them towards the treasures ahead. At Arica there was disappointment; three little vessels produced but a hundredweight of silver, but they had news of a well-loaded ship to the north. So on, in chase, only to find her at anchor with her silver hidden ashore. How they cursed! Some fool had set a light to a ship at Arica without orders, thus giving an advertisement of their coming. They made all sail on the deserted ship and let her drive masterless into the great ocean to fetch up God knows where, while the *Golden Hind* herself stood for Callao de Lima.

And coming towards that port one evening, Drake met a ship outward-bound from which he took, willy nilly, a pilot, by whose assistance, that same night, he slipped into the harbor to find a fair crowd of shipping, the watchmen asleep, the crews ashore carousing. After some quiet searching in the dark, his people found a quantity of silk and fine linen and a chest chock-full of royals of plate. Unfortunately, a Spaniard, pulling around the harbor and noticing some movement on board, hailed the stranger and had for answer, "The *Michael Angelo* of Chile." Unsuspecting, and looking for a drink — waterside folk were ever thirsty souls — the man came on board, only to jump quickly into his boat again, yelling, "Hell and pirates!" For in the gloom he had seen a cannon's mouth. Presently there was uproar, which steadily increased as Drake's men cut the cables, so that ships were driving and smashing helplessly about the harbor, much of their rigging hacked to pieces. As soon as the *Golden Hind* could collect her men, she weighed, and the last ruffle before the dawn took her clear of the harbor. In this affair one Englishman was shot, the second and the last to fall to the Spaniards.

As the sun rose, the breeze fell away to a flat calm and the *Golden Hind* lay still in the sight of the town. It was not, however, the approach of the two ship-loads of soldiers which emerged from the harbor that worried the Englishmen so much as the thought that a ship which they had just heard of from a prisoner was probably increasing an already long lead. The name of this ship, they learned, was the *Nuestra Señora de la Concepción*, her captain San Juan de Anton, her destination Panama, her cargo the King of Spain's treasure. She had left Callao a fortnight before but, as she was calling at Paita, there was hope that she might be overtaken before reaching the golden city. Fortunately for the Spanish soldiers, who had no cannon, a breeze sprang up before their boats came within range of the English ship's battery or there would have been a sad slaughter. The sea darkened under the freshing southerly wind, all sail was crowded on the ship and away she flew in chase — a heavy handicap, but thirteen hundred miles to go.

At Paita, where they picked up a prize, they learned that the chase had dallied, and they knew that they were gaining hand over fist; the wind failed under the Line, but on they went with sweeps out and the pinnace towing ahead. Prizes they met, which gave them silks and silver lamps and such like gauds, a great golden crucifix, and a chest of wrought plate; but it was news of how the chase fared that interested them more now, for every one of those fifty-six sunburnt seamen knew that ahead was the ship which might make good their captain's promise that they all would one day live as right good gentlemen in England. Kuph! How they sweated under the boiling tropic sun in that molten copper sea. As they swept past Guayaquil they learned that their quarry was just over the sea rim; the wind freshened again, and next morning, nearing Cape San Francisco, Captain Drake promised his golden chain, whereon hung his whistle, to the man who should first sight the chase, and not long after came a hail from the main topgallant yard: "A sail broad on the larboard bow!"

And there, sure enough, she was. But the wary gentleman who commanded the *Golden Hind* was taking no chances, he had no intention of frightening the golden bird, he did not wish any fluttering, he did not wish her to lose a single feather, but purposed taking her comfortably at nightfall. So, putting out drogues in the shape of empty wine jars, to reduce his speed, his crew spent the long afternoon lying on deck with their arms beside them, talking of how they would spend their money. To them, as to most seamen who make long passages on hard bread and salt meat, Heaven was to be a place of unlimited fresh food and drink; in this West Country ship life would be all Devonshire cream, apples and hogsheads of cider, up along and down along, and there was to be no more sea. Meanwhile, below in his cabin, Francis Drake dressed himself with meticulous care for the evening's performance.

As the sun slanted, the chase stood towards them for company — the sea is a lonely place. As it sank and the darkness fell, the two ships closed. Drake sent some of his men into the pinnace which was towing alongside, and cutting adrift his drogues, passed under the stern of the *Nuestra Señora*. There was silence save for the gentle *slap slap* of the water under the bows and buttocks of the two slow-moving ships. Then a cheery, "What ship is that?" from the Spaniard, and answer, "the *Michael Angelo*." With that the *Golden Hind* ranged alongside and a clear voice rang out, "Strike Señor Juan de Anton, unless you would be sent to the bottom!"

"Strike?" thundered the Biscayan sailor. "What kind of a cruet stand do you take this for to strike to you?"

And now, at last realizing into what company he had fallen, he sprang to the helm, hoping to get his ship free. It was too late. A *sho-o-oh* of arrows and a crash of shot sent his crew scurrying below, the pinnace boarded on his disengaged side, and he, alone and without so much as a rapier to defend himself, could do nought else but surrender. Captain Drake, in a magnificent suit of armor, received his prisoner on the deck of the *Golden Hind*, showing him great kindness, which no doubt softened a little the hardness of his case.

The ships were brought on a westerly course for thirty-six hours, and when it was considered that they had reached a position which was safe from interruption, the great pillage began. Hour after hour Anton, sitting below, heard the rattle and thud of the hoists of silver bars and treasure chests as they were lowered on board. At one hatch, a gang was getting up ballast, and sand from Devon beaches was going overboard into the Pacific to make room for the precious metal. There were twenty-six tons of silver in bar alone, thirteen great chests of pieces of eight, nearly a hundredweight of gold. The deck was a litter of jewels and plate. Every corner of the ship was rummaged — be sure the golden bird was well plucked.

This was Master Francis Drake's cargo of currants, to fetch which he had set out from Plymouth.

The Spaniards were now put again into their gutted ship, each with a little present of money. To the captain, Drake gave a valuable piece of armor and a German firelock besides a safe conduct or sort of letter of introduction, in case he should fall in with Captain Winter, who, Drake supposed, might still be in the South Sea. The letter was written in terms of piety, and contained doctrines which commended themselves to the Englishman, which it may be supposed he hoped the Spaniard might find helpful, "together with the chastening he had received," in seeing the "errors of the Catholic religion." Poor Captain Anton! The treasure ship, in ballast, made the best of her way into Panama, while the heavily laden

Golden Hind steered northwest. A few more prizes came her way, a few more golden ornaments, a ship full of silks and satins, of rare spices and drugs, of velvets and damasks — excellent dunnage for the more valuable chinaware and delicate jewels of the Collection. Last of all, one moonlit night, they came upon a prize which gave them a set of Spanish charts of the Pacific to guide the rovers homeward.

By this time the whole Pacific Coast had rubbed its eyes and was awake. The Viceroy of Peru made haste to cast six cannon, mounting them in two ships which came twenty days late at Cape San Francisco; the Bishop of Guatemala was melting down his cathedral bells to make more cannon; Don Martin Enriquez, Viceroy of Mexico, was drilling men, horse and foot, white and brown, marching them up hill and down again; ships were sailing hard to the southward to bar the way through Magellan Straits; messengers were hastening over the Isthmus to Nombre de Dios and Old Spain with the news. There was, as Drake's men would say, "the Devil to pay and no pitch hot."

And the *Golden Hind* — considerably less than a hundred feet over all — stood away far to the northward into unknown seas, and then made herself small for a while in a haven nearby where now stands the noble City of San Francisco.

Across the wide and stormy ocean, which men call Pacific, they sailed homeward-bound, past the Isle of Thieves to Mindanao, south among many islands to meet strange kings, and on to what might once have been some dusky Calypso's isle, so beautiful it was. Here the little ship lay refitting for a month beneath the branches of gigantic trees which towered high above her masthead.

Refreshed with delicious fruits, they sailed again, but not long after crashed upon a sunken reef, where all seemed lost and the ship's bell tolled for prayers and a sermon from the chaplain. When, after great exertions, the ship was refloated and came clear, the captain remembered the sermon, which had struck him as a little too pointed in parts, so fitting himself out as the Pope and sitting solemnly on deck, he there excommunicated his chaplain from the Church, consigning him to the devil and all his angels. (The Queen thought this very wicked of her versatile sailor — but she laughed a little, too.) Once clear of the tangle of islands and coral reefs of the East Indies, the *Golden Hind* made a most happy passage around the Cape of Good Hope to Sierra Leone, whence, after filling her water casks for the last time, she set sail for England.

As Drake finished his story, of which here is but a faded outline, the late October day was ending; the firelight shone on the Queen's face and illumined the little piles of damasks and eastern embroideries, and silks with fantastic figurings, which lay at her feet; and William Cecil, Lord Burghley, entering to lay before his Royal Mistress a document of State, noticed in the lady's lap a little heap of jewels. As Elizabeth pretended to read, she noticed that the sailor proffered a golden trinket to the Lord Treasurer, but the Lord Treasurer of England looked out of the window and said not a word. The rebuff did not worry the seaman, though it made the Queen think, and the great Lord Burghley withdrew, leaving the lady thinking. A jewel glittered in the firelight, Elizabeth thought again, and — as you know — made a knight of Francis Drake.

It seems strange that there should be no authentic dimensions of the *Golden Hind* preserved, considering she remained for nearly one hundred years in dry dock as one of the sights of London after her return from the circumnavigation. An estimate of her size arrived at by the measurement of the bricks used in building her dock at Deptford gives 75 feet L.O.A., 60 feet L.B.P., 47 feet keel, 19 feet beam, and 9 feet or 10 feet depth. On the other hand, it is said that she once paid dues on 150 tons, which was presumably her gross tonnage, and this would mean about 113 tons burden. By giving her three more feet of beam and another foot of depth, we would bring her nearer to the usual proportions of a merchantship, and by using 100 as a divisor would have $113\frac{74}{100}$ tons, a small enough ship in which to preserve in good health 56 men for a period of three years. I should think that her dimensions are likely to have been: Length between perpendiculars, 65 feet, keel 47 feet, beam 22 feet, and depth in hold 11 feet, but there was no standard arithmetical system of tonnage measurement in England before 1582, and for some years afterwards Thames merchant shipbuilders measured for beam and depth outside the planking and divided by 94, while Government yards measured inside the planking and divided by 100.

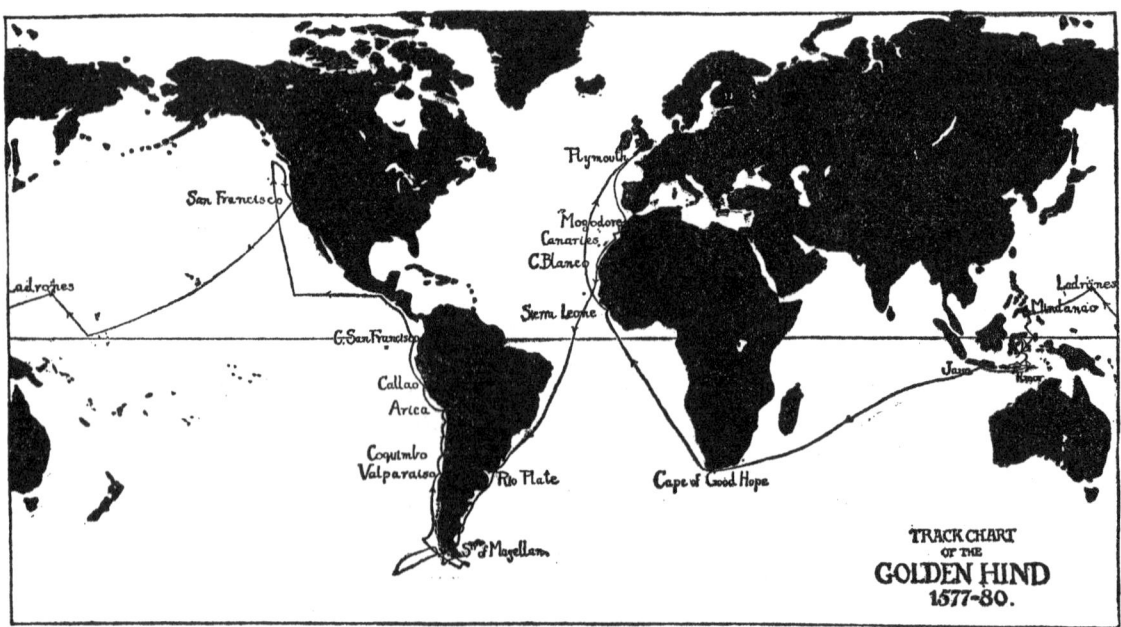

TRACK CHART OF THE GOLDEN HIND 1577-80.

V
THE REVENGE

THE REVENGE, 1591

THE REVENGE

The Battle of the Azores in 1591 When a Single Ship Defied a Fleet

VIEWED from any great height, the sea takes on an appearance of unreality. The roughest waves seem ironed out flat, the color of the water deepens and fades mysteriously in patches as the shadows of clouds pass over it. Ships, even great ships, look as toys, as little models, which one might pick up off the colored board and play with; they move, but their movement is as imperceptible as that of the hands of a clock. There is silence. All is as unlike the sea which the sailor uses as it can be.

Had one been standing high up on the Island of Flores in the Azores on the last day of August, 1591, the sum of this unreality would have been added to by the curious maneuvers of the ships below; they were inexplicable. Well away on the brightly painted board, out to the westward was an ordered group of ships with yards square, their heads towards the passage between Flores and the Isle of Corvo to the north. Fifty-three ships one might count, perhaps fifty-five. A keen eye could detect that they bore the flag of Spain. A group of twelve, only four of which were ships of force, was standing close hauled on the starboard tack with their heads as near SW as they could lie; these flew white flags with the red St. George's cross of England, and already they had a good offing. Nearer — she had come out late from under the cliffs — was a smart looking ship flying the flags and pendants of St. George, too; she was on the port tack and under easy sail. Close to her was a small vessel flying the George, following like a short legged faithful dog.

With half an eye it could be seen that the line of advance of the ship on the port tack intersected the line of the approaching fleet; if things kept going as they were, she would fetch up about the middle of the bunch. On the other hand, the twelve away on the starboard tack looked to be holding so good a wind that one might judge they would weather the fleet when they flung round. That was the first puzzle. Why did the fleet let the twelve get the weather gauge? But that was an easier problem than that of the near ship. There was a war on. Was she putting on a brag, was it a bluff, and would she up helm and run for it while there was time? She was leaving it pretty late, for puffs of smoke came from the wing ships of the fleet and white splashes were all around her. Then the little vessel came close under the lee, hung there for a moment, then eased sheets and ran down wind. The lonely ship held on. After a while the observer would have seen a puff of smoke come from her port bow, a second or two and the boom of a big gun. At that the sea birds on the outlying rocks got up and screamed a protest. It was three o'clock and a fine afternoon. Followed a regular thunder of guns and much smoke till all around was covered as with a pall.

Had it been possible to get within hail of the small vessel on her way down wind, her captain could not have given much explanation. Certainly he would have told you that the ship from which he had just parted was the *Revenge* with Sir Richard Grenville on board and he would have said that he was the victualler attached to her; that when she had got under way he had heard a great bobbery going on aboard — hard swearing and such — so that he could get no orders. He had, therefore, followed until hailed to get to blazes out of it. But that old skipper would have said that he was beat, befogged and bewildered as to the reason of it all; yes, completely befogged.

On board the *Revenge* men moved smartly for there was much to do and she was short-handed. A good few were away in prizes, ninety sick were lying on the ballast in the hold, many of them quite helpless; so that every fit man was doing the work of two. The boatswain forward was short-handed securing the anchors, the master was short-handed trimming the sails, while below the master gunner was getting the last ounce out of his crowd as they loaded, rammed home, and ran out the guns with the tackles — demi-cannon with their 32-pound, cannon-perrier with 24-pound, and culverin with 18-pound shot; while in her upper tier were demi-culverins, sakers, falcons; with portpieces, fowlers, and bases above for quick-firers. Small arm men made ready their pieces, pikes, axes, pots of lime, pots of hard yellow peas soaked in tallow to send rolling about her decks and send rolling to any who had the temerity to board and the misfortune to step upon these. The carpenter and his mates contributed in the shape of long boards with spikes which they secured along the rail, false hatches which hinged downwards and let a man on to waiting pikes below. They made ready as well sheets of lead, pitch, planks, nails, and canvas for patches and quick repairs. Among the seamen there was no time for cogitation, speculation or any other fancy work of the brain but, as is their habit, they found in expectoration a satisfying substitute.

Beside the ensign on the poop stood the gaily clad trumpeters, collectively known as the ship's *Noise*. In those days the word had not the derogatory sense it has since acquired; however, had we heard them as they tuned up on that hot afternoon, we might perhaps have thought the modern sense fitted well.

Over all these brawny sweating men waved the long streamer of St. George which occasionally came foul of a brace or backstay, only to flick itself clear and proudly flaunt again in the sunshine; while below in the hold, well below the water line, by the dim light of a purser's farthing dip, the surgeon looked to his knives and quietly counted his tourniquets.

Such was the manner in which a ship was prepared for battle in the days of

Good Queen Bess, and so doubtless the *Revenge* made ready on that memorable day.

Had we gone on board I do not think we should have had much difficulty in identifying Sir Richard Grenville. He stood alone. A man of large estate ashore, a keen rider to hounds, he carried early habit to sea when he chose to go, which he had done for many years intermittently. A good horse would carry a man anywhere and he looked to his ship to do the like. He never thought deep and he never thought twice.

As they closed, he could not but have admired the fine order of the approaching fleet and, nearer yet, he must have found himself counting the rows of cannon and like enough as he did so — being the man he was — he laughed. If he glanced sideways towards the master of his ship to see if he were counting too, it was to meet disappointment.

As soon as the Spaniards had appeared over the horizon in regular formation, that old seaman had made up his reckoning of guns and all; now, with eye glued to the weather clue of the topsail, he had no other thought but to keep his ship going. That was his business and, beyond an occasional "No near-r" or a "Keep her full" to the man at the helm, he had nought to say; there was nothing more to be said.

An Elizabethan

There came an interval of complete silence save for the slap and swish and popple of the water along the ship's side. Then came the boom of a gun and the splash of a random shot from the fleet. Another silence. Then from the master gunner below a "Keep her so" — a pause, and then in voice of thunder: "Fire!" The cannon-perrier on the weather bow of the *Revenge* crashed forth and shook the whole ship; the smoke and smell of burnt powder blew back into men's faces, half choking the trumpeters and causing appalling variations in the tune of defiance which at that moment was being given forth at full blast.

As to what happened during the next fifteen hours no man afterwards told the same tale. In all violent actions the field of vision is limited, the sense of time is lost and it is hard to regain the sequence of events, only the onset and the end coming clear again to the mind. There was the memory of the Spaniards hauling their wind, a picture of ships in bright sunlight seen through the ports of the darkened lower deck of the *Revenge;* of a single galleon shaking up, with sheets and tacks flying, and falling in disorder to leeward; of the first rattle and bang of blocks and gear from aloft; of the first raking broad-side which came crashing and splintering through the stern. After that, confusion. Memories of heavy crashes as masts fell, a blinding flash as a culverin exploded in loading, the thud of a carriage capsizing, all mixed in with such trivialities as the picking up of a chain and locket which had slipped from a man's neck, the retieing of a handkerchief round a fellow's head, of the shot that put "paid" to the galley funnel. A memory of the heavy lurch as the first ship came bumping and grinding alongside, tearing off port lids and channels. The cry of "repel boarders" and the tumbling up into clean air from the sulphurous choking atmosphere below — a change from the heavy labor of shifting artillery to a quick hack and thrust and thrust, and then back to labor again. Of more ships blundering alongside and the realization that the sun had not stood still, was dipping; then the night and the memory of ships sinking alongside or disappearing into the darkness.

It is likely all would have held in remembrance one staggering shock. It was the last hope of the overwhelmed ship, when her upper deck was in possession of the enemy, to collect kegs of gunpowder, lay a train and blow it and them sky high. This device was recommended when valiant and determined men could be found to undertake it. There were valiant and determined men in the *Revenge* that night.

Certain it is that as the night wore on the ship was left more to herself and she suffered no more than an occasional distant cannonading, to be answered now and again with one of her few remaining guns, as though, unable to do more, she spat defiance. A little before dawn came a silence. There was time to look around.

The carpenter reported six feet of water in the hold; indeed, the seamen knew it for the easy motion had passed and she lurched like a drunken man, sure sign of a waterlogged ship. As the water had risen it had put an end to the pains of the more helpless while the rest of the sick had dragged themselves to where it was dry. The surgeon had been killed about midnight while attending Sir Richard on deck; his boy made shift to do what he could for the wounded below. At the best of times in these old ships a man went with bent head and wary feet; in that dark hour, with no more than the light of a horn lantern, movement was slow along her main orlop. But there was light enough for some things that had been better shrouded. Weird patterns traced about the deck as though black ink had been spilt and a man could not keep his feet clear of it. Dismounted guns slid and stopped and slid, splinters lay everywhere on deck, and jagged splinters from beams threatened from above. Men lay moaning and crying for water in the shadows. Here lay what was a friend and there a man with whom one knew he had quarreled about something — well, about nothing, as most quarrels are in small ships long from the land. Their accounts were settled now, anyway.

Under the stars lay Sir Richard Grenville, alive but desperately wounded. It is while he lay in this condition that the popular story gives to his part a long and florid speech. Men of his caliber at any time are short of words, and at this pass it is hard to believe that he would have said much. But it would be certainly in keeping with his character that he would have briefly ordered the ship to be blown up, and doubtless had he been able he would himself have carried it out. But the master-gunner, to whom perforce he entrusted the work, seems to have been a talker; he let it be known what he was going to do; one suspects he was not quite so resolute as the story would have us believe. At any rate it is certain that the master of the *Revenge* now took a leading part and clapped the fellow under arrest, determining that he himself and the others who were not mortally wounded might have chance of life; he went on board the Spanish admiral with an offer of surrender on condition of life and liberty. Curiosity was probably mixed with admiration — curiosity to know the reason for a seemingly mad adventure and admiration for gallantry in defense beyond all experience. Don Alonzo de Bazan accepted the surrender on terms, sending a boat to bring Sir Richard on board, where he was received with honor and treated with gentleness till his death a few days afterwards. To this period, when he lay dying, is given another long speech in which, after praising his own conduct, he cursed those of his comrades whom he considered had deserted in battle. There is, however, another account which states that, from the time of his being carried on board the Spanish flagship until his death, Sir Richard Grenville never once opened his lips. That seems to be more credible and a happier ending for any man.

We may believe that the master surrendered what he supposed was a doomed ship — she seemed battered and strained beyond hope. He left out of his reckoning the 7,000 odd men in Bazan's fleet besides a few thousand more in the West

Indian Convoy which arrived at Corvo two days after the fight. With so many hands to draw upon, it was possible to clear the *Revenge* of water and make her reasonably tight for the voyage to Spain. How the day of her arrival was looked forward to we can imagine when we remember that the whole country was still smarting under the humiliation of 1588, and here was coming in as prize the ship which had borne the flag of Sir Francis Drake against the Great Armada.

In his old age Admiral Sir William Monson recalled the sorrowfulest sight ever he saw. He, with others, had been captured when in charge of Spanish prizes and were held prisoners in Lisbon Castle. One morning, being upon the walls with a guard of soldiers, he says, "We beheld a great galleon of the King of Spain's turning up the river in her fighting sails, being sumptuously decked with ensigns, streamers and pendants, with all other ornaments to show her bravery; she let fly all her ordnance in a triumphant manner for the taking of Sir Richard Grenville in the *Revenge* at the island of Flores, she being one of the fleet." But that galleon brought no trophy in her wake.For, not long after the great fight, in a gale of wind, the *Revenge* had gone down.

Sir Walter Raleigh's *True Report* is the chief authority upon which the generally accepted story is based and Tennyson's ballad is Raleigh's prose turned into verse, owing little to any other source. Raleigh was Grenville's kinsman, believing in him while others did not; so that the *Report* must be read as the generous defense of the memory of his friend whom he praises without abusing others — a rare thing in this class of literature but Raleigh was above all a gentleman. It was, besides, a strong piece of war propaganda and a religious tract written by one of the greatest prose writers of all time. We may expect, therefore, a little embroidery. Nevertheless, other accounts, although they disagree as to the events leading up to the action, detract little from the splendor of the defense as related by Raleigh.

Lord Thomas Howard, with Grenville as his vice admiral, had been sent out to intercept the West India Convoy in April and in August he was still waiting. In the meantime, disease had broken out in the squadron and he had received warning from home that a large fleet was preparing in Spain to escort the convoy from the Azores. He hung on in hopes that the merchantmen would arrive first; towards the end of the month he was forced to anchor at Flores so that he might shift and clean his ballast, fill up with water and give his men a run ashore.

An English squadron, stationed off the Portuguese coast under the Earl of Cumberland, sighted the armada soon after it had left Ferrol. Cumberland kept away but ordered the *Moonshine* to dog the Spaniards and, as soon as she was certain of their destination, to carry on and warn Howard. The *Moonshine*, which was a handy little packet, dodged about on the horizon and, as soon as she realized they intended first for Angra, clapped on all she could carry and bolted for Flores.

Raleigh states that she "had no sooner delivered the news but the fleet was in sight," Monson says the *Moonshine* had come in the night before. Remembering that Raleigh was out to defend his friend, we need not see here a flat contradiction. With the long warning and the short, there should have been no surprise. But a contemporary Spanish historian wrote that Alonzo made an approach from the westward with the hope that he would be mistaken for the convoy. Monson says that Howard was in doubt as to what the fleet was and therefore worked out to windward until he was sure, while Grenville decided forthwith that it was the convoy. The master warned him that they were not merchantmen out to windward and advised him to make sail while he might and rejoin the Admiral when he could. This advice was rejected and the master threatened with violence if he gave any more of it.

There is no doubt that Grenville, for some reason, was unable to get away as soon as the other ships, though it is equally sure that it was open to him to run to leeward had he chosen. Some accounts say he had his sick ashore and out of compassion for them he delayed, and then they go on to say "out of the greatness of his mind" he decided to sail slap through the Spanish fleet, forgetting for the moment his compassion for the sick.

There have been many attempts to explain Grenville's conduct. It has been suggested that he was a disappointed man and deliberately decided to make an end. Certainly he had often been thwarted. Nearly twenty years before he had projected an expedition into the Pacific and, after his commission had been drawn up, the expedition had been stayed. Within a year or two he was to see Drake, who had been selected to lead a similar adventure, carry it through and thereby rise to fame. In 1585 Raleigh chose Grenville as his representative in the first attempt to found Virginia. On the way he wasted time and substance by a digression, attacking the Spanish colonies in the West Indies before he planted his people. Before he returned to them with supplies, these people had lost heart and accepted Drake's offer of a passage home again, so that he returned only to find a deserted colony. On this second visit to America, he left behind fifty men to the mercy of the Indians whom he had already antagonised by ruthless punishment, having burnt a town because an individual had stolen a silver cup. It is not surprising that these fifty men were never heard of again. In 1588 he had been entrusted with the organization of the second line of defense in the West Country which was never called upon, the first line having done the Spaniards' business in the Channel. To a man of his fighting spirit, this must have been trouble enough. Yes, although he had made much money privateering, he was a man of disappointments. But it is incredible that he could have been so base as to deliberately fling away one of Her Majesty's ships together with the lives of his comrades merely to add to the picturesqueness of his own end.

It is certainly kinder to accept Sir William Monson's judgment. The man made a mistake. That, after having discovered his error, he chose to see the business through in an optimistic mood is credible, but it is more likely that the error was not discovered until he was jammed and could not get clear. Monson says that he endeavored to escape, but too late.

But perhaps you think that, in spite of the fact that they were decimated with disease, in spite of all, the four men-of-war *Defiance, Lion, Bonaventure* and *Foresight* might have done more than make a demonstration after they had got clear to windward; that Howard, Sir Robert Crosse, old George Fenner and Vavasour, men who both before and after fought for their country with gallantry, ought to have stood by Sir Richard Grenville. Very well.

On September 22nd, 1914, three British cruisers, *Hogue, Cressy* and *Aboukir*, were patroling in the North Sea. One was hit by a torpedo fired from a German submarine, the other two stopped to pick up survivors; they too were torpedoed. Fourteen hundred men were lost when those three ships went down. The British Admiralty issued an order to the fleet that in future when a ship was torpedoed that ship was to be left to her fate. I do not know the date of the order but suspect it was September 23rd, 1914.

On the night of January 1st, 1915, a fleet was steaming up the English Channel and H.M.S. *Formidable* was hit. Captain Loxley was on the bridge; he called a signalman. "Make," said he, "I have been torpedoed." The signalman went to his key and tapped out the message. The flagship flashed back the letters R.D. ·—· —··, which is only to say: "Your signal is read and understood." Loxley knew the signal would be understood. The fleet steamed away. The *Formidable* turned over and sank. It was midwinter, the weather was bad. There were no speeches, no reproaches, and no music, except the tap of the signalman's key.

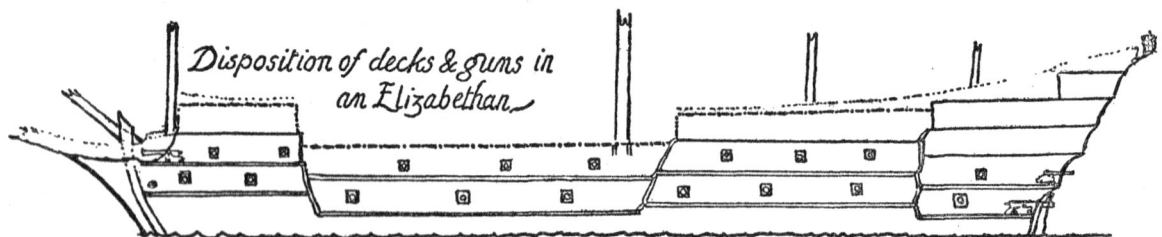

Disposition of decks & guns in an Elizabethan

VI
THE SUSAN CONSTANT

THE SUSAN CONSTANT, 1607

THE SUSAN CONSTANT

*She Carried to Jamestown the First Colonists from
England for Virginia*

THE COUNCIL of the Virginia Company of London sat around a table at the Treasurer's house in Philpot Lane with a map of the Northern Hemisphere spread out before them. There had been difficulty in finding money for a sixth attempt to make a lodgment in North America. Sir Walter Raleigh had spent a small fortune while Queen Elizabeth had given the country a good name all to no purpose, and therefore it was not surprising that, after five failures, the project had come to be reckoned a wild cat scheme by the cautious.

But by the latter end of 1606 the Council had succeeded in enticing enough money to charter three small ships and there had been no difficulty in filling the vessels brimming over with the less cautious of mankind. They had been fortunate, too, in obtaining the services of Captain Christopher Newport as admiral of the expedition and, one day in chill December, that bright-eyed trusty mariner was in attendance to take into his custody a sealed box — to be opened only on arrival in Virginia — containing the names of those who were to have the government of the new country.

He was also present so that he might hear read over "The instructions by way of advice to the settlers" which contained a deal of common sense about their trade with and their conduct towards the Indians, and the building up of their new home. Houses for the common wealth were to be built before houses for private wealth and use and, "seeing that order is at the same price with confusion," their houses were to be set even and in a line, giving good breadth to the streets, which were to be carried square about the market place. "Lastly and chiefly the way to prosper and achieve good success is to make yourselves all of one mind for the good of your country and your own, and to serve and fear God the giver of all goodness, for every plantation which our Heavenly Father hath not planted shall be rooted out." To all of which we may be sure the good Captain murmured "Amen."

But the advice which concerned him more particularly was in the opening paragraph and, although with our present knowledge it raises a smile, to those who had written it in foggy old London in 1606, with an eye on the map lying on the table, it seemed reasonable enough. Briefly, the settlers were ordered to choose a river tending to the NW for thereby they would more quickly reach the other sea (which was the Pacific) and thus on to the riches of the East. So we see that, more than a hundred years after discovery, America for many was still hardly worth while except as a half-way house. By their map the Gulf of California bent round obligingly and shot through the Rockies, through Arizona, Colorado, Kansas, past Missouri into Kentucky; while from the Atlantic seaboard an arm reached into the land towards a great lake away down in Tennessee, which same lake was a reservoir for the two oceans in case they should run dry.

So Captain Newport, having paid his respects to the Council, tucked the mystery box and the bundle of advice under his arm and went on board his flagship *Susan Constant*, lying with the *Godspeed* and the pinnace off Blackwall. His passengers were all on board; the last farewells were said; they cleared the ship and shortened in and at the ebb fell down the Thames, among all the ships carrying everything from everywhere, bound out and bound in. But though they had the will to go the wind would have them stay, and for three weeks and more they were in the Downs waiting for a shift. Here Captain Newport had time to weigh up his passengers, and those passengers could not help but learn to know one another, for the two ends of the promenade deck were precious close together. All told there were something like 160 of them distributed in the three ships, about 50 of whom were styled gentlemen, many of them very young.

There was Edward Wingfield, scholarly and dignified, who had seen service as a soldier in Ireland, holding somewhat aloof from the rest. Captain Bartholomew Gosnold, who had been in America a few years before and had written "Martha's Vineyard" on the map; believing in the new country himself and being a likeable man, he, more than anyone else, was the means of bringing about the present expedition. There was Gabriel Archer, pernickety, litigious and pushful. Radcliffe, whose attempt at concealment that his real name was Sicklemore seemed to make him thin (he looked as though he had tossed for his breakfast and lost); while Edward Brookes, as round as a barrel, certainly looked as though he had always won. Alas! poor Edward was never to reach Virginia, for in the hot sun of the West Indies "the fat melted within him," and he died. Then there was a full-bearded forceful man who, although he was only eight and twenty, had seen more of adventure (according to his own account) than all the rest of the company put together; his name was John Smith; George Percy, younger brother to the Earl of Northumberland, who was later to become President of the Council, and many other young hopefuls who are but names. For the building of the new town there were four carpenters, two bricklayers and a mason; a dozen laborers for the fields, a blacksmith, a barber, and George Love the tailor — few whole suitings but many a patch he was afterwards to put in at his little shop in James Town; Nicolas Scot, keeping his drum as dry as he could in the ship so that he might roll and rattle it on occasions of state; finally, the Reverend Edward Hunt came as shepherd to a somewhat wayward flock.

It was the end of January, 1607, before they saw the last of England and, with a fair wind, turned south for the Canaries; here they completed with wood and water, after four or five days standing away for the West Indies. It was soon after leaving the Canary Islands that Captain John Smith got into trouble. It is likely enough that close confinement, heavy food and unaccustomed heat told on many of those who were making a first voyage, though the inconveniences would have had little effect on an old hand, so that Smith's exuberances were not abated while the others became limp and miserable and suffered from what we now call an inferiority complex. The oft-told tale of his decapitating three Turks (evidence of which was displayed in his coat of arms), besides success in other combats, began to scare the more timid, and as, had he wished, he could have bested them, so, they imagined, he would. Hence arose the idea that he intended in the new country to put up with no councils but rule as king. I do not suppose that men like Gosnold were afraid of him and certainly Captain Newport was not, though both may have found his tales boring and perhaps his table manners none of the best. So, for the sake of peace and comfort amongst the passengers, John Smith was put under arrest. It does not seem credible that he ever had any evil intent or ambition. The worst that we might say of him is that he was a bit of a blowhard and that in his blowing he did not find time to give credit to others who may have had the same end in view but were following a different route. Of course, hero worshippers in the past have made a fool of him — as they ever do — but it does seem to me that those scholarly American writers who have written him down as a mere charlatan are at fault and treat a little ungenerously a brave man and a robust who, when the need was, gave of his best to Virginia.

On March 23rd the little fleet raised Martinique out of the blue and on the following day anchored under Dominica, where English laborers and bricklayers saw at close quarters real live cannibals with their bodies all painted red to keep away the biting of the "musketos;" where they saw a thrasher and a swordfish fight a whale, and a hundred other things very strange to behold. Then they sailed past Mariagalanta to Guadeloupe, where Newport showed them a bath so hot that it boiled a leg of pork; sailing by Montserrat and St. Christopher, they came to Nevis where all the men were landed and camped for six days beside mineral springs, and here, with fresh food and good exercise, the troubles of the voyage passed from memory.

By April 4th they were at the Virgin Islands, catching fish and boiling turtle soup. On the 7th they were at Mona for water; it was there they left stout Edward Brookes. An afternoon's excursion to the little island of Monica, bird's-nesting on a large scale — they came away with two boatloads of eggs — brought their holiday to an end and on the 10th of April "they disimboged out of the West Indies and bear a course northerly."

Christopher Newport had been able to give them all a good time. In his younger days, as Captain in the *Golden Dragon*, he had taken Yaguana and Ocoa in San Domingo and Truxillo in Honduras, besides nineteen prizes in one trip, and had been one of that fortunate band who took the great *Madre de Dios* in 1592, when many a seaman came home with a capful of rubies while their lady loves went in brocades intended for princesses. He knew the West Indies inside out and so was able to take his passengers to the best places for health and entertainment, just as though he were conducting a pleasure cruise in a liner. Nowadays, in the city on James River which bears his name, they build bigger ships than the *Susan Constant*, with better accommodation, but they fare far before they find a better man to command any one of them than Christopher Newport.

On April 21st, by which time they were hoping for a landfall, there piped up the noisy overture to the settlement of Virginia. At five o'clock that evening they were hit by a "vehement tempest," butt end first. Thunder crash, lightning, rain and wind, so that they were forced to lie "ahull" with poor Radcliffe in the pinnace wishing for home. Then for four days they used the lead without finding bottom, but at daylight on the morning of the 26th from the masthead came the welcome call "Land ho!" Later in the day, passing a point which they named Cape Henry, they entered the Chesapeake to anchor under Old Point Comfort, one hundred and twenty-seven days out from London River. That night, in Captain Newport's cabin, was opened the sealed box. The scene was set; the curtain was up for the first act in the American drama.

We know how, quite early in the proceedings, Captain Newport sailed up James River looking optimistically for that lake which he expected might bring them all well on the way to the Pacific. We know the Virginians treated much of the good advice given as such advice is often treated; how there was forgetfulness that order is at the same price as confusion, and how houses came to be built anyhow and not square about the market place. How they were soon at loggerheads and not all of one mind, and how they neglected the more serious duties enjoined in their instructions. But all this is the way of youth and for the strong, who are able to bear the hard kicks of experience. 'Tis better so; a deep scar is a more lasting reminder than many good words out of musty books.

The early hopes, trials and successes are written at large in the shore-going history books; while the touching story of Pocohontas; the wonders of the seasons in this new country; the bright silveriness of the Chesapeake; the twilight and deep mystery of the woods; the elusiveness, with the sudden and terrible appearance of the Indians, are as an inexhaustible well from which writers of romance ever draw inspiration. Christopher Newport at that first coming had some difficulty in tearing himself away from it all, but he was of the sea and go he must. Our business being in deep waters too, we must go with him.

It seems right to give here as a sort of footnote something of the contemporary seaman's views of the ship and her way in the sea, so that it will be clear where nautical knowledge stood at this dawning of the history of the United States, and folk may the better understand how far they have progressed in the three hundred odd years.

Fortunately, there were three men who wrote on the subject at this time and, strangely enough, all had some connection with Virginia.

First, the great Captain John Smith himself has left behind his *Seaman's Grammar;* secondly, Captain Nathaniel Butler, Governor of Bermuda in 1620 and leader of an expedition against the Chickahominy Indians in 1622, who left behind his *Dialogical Discourses between a Captain and an Admiral;* this is a great deal fuller than Smith's work. Lastly, Sir Henry Mainwaring who, though never nearer Virginia than Newfoundland — and there it must be confessed only in the shady part of a pirate — later, in his regenerate days, became a member of the Virginia Company. He wrote the *Seaman's Dictionary.* Smith and Butler were both soldier captains who eventually went to sea, while Mainwaring was first and last a seaman, though incidentally a B.A., Camb.; M.D., Oxon.; student of the Inner Temple; Gentleman of the Bedchamber to King James I; Lieutenant of Dover Castle; Deputy Lord Warden of the Cinque Ports, and a respectable Admiral in the Royal Navy, besides having been in his youth of that profession which has been already reluctantly mentioned. He wrote to make people understand, while Smith and Butler wrote more because they liked writing. Mainwaring is the best to quote, therefore, and here, strung together out of his *Dictionary,* are Mainwaring's views about the form of a ship:

"The bow is of great importance for this first breaks the sea and is that part which bears all the ship forward on when she is pressed down with sail, which is in a manner the bearing of the ship. If the bow be too broad the ship will not pass easily through the sea but carry a great deal of dead water before her; if it be too lean or thin, she will pitch or beat mightily into a hollow sea for want of breadth to bear her up, so that there must be a discreet mean betwixt both these. The shaping of this part doth much import the ship's going by a wind; yet I have seen both sorts go well by a wind, but most commonly those that have good bold bows; nevertheless it is certain that a ship's way after on — which is called her run — is of more importance for her sailing by a wind. The run is of main importance for the ship's sailing, for if the water come not swiftly to the rudder she will never steer well, and it is a general observation that a ship that doth not steer well will not sail well, and then she cannot keep a good wind, for if a ship hath not fresh way through the sea she must needs fall to leeward with the sea. We say a ship hath a good run when it is long and cometh off handsomely by degrees, and a bad run when it is short and that the ship is too full below.

"The rake of a ship is so much of her hull as doth overhang both ends of the keel. A great rake forward gives a ship good way and makes her keep a good wind, but if she have not a good full bow it will make her pitch mightily into the head sea; the longer the rake the fuller must be the bow and the best conditioned ships have neither too much nor too little. The rake aft being of no use to the ship but only to make her ship shapen (as they call it) they give as little as may be.

"The rudder is the bridle which governs the ship and the narrower it is the better, if the ship do feel it; for a broad rudder doth hold much dead water if the helm be put over to any side; but if the ship hath a fat quarter so that the water cannot come quick and strong to the rudder, then she will require a broad rudder."

Allowing for a few old-fashioned words and phrases, that does not seem very different from the introduction to a primer on hull form which might be written today. Of the trim of a ship Mainwaring goes on to say:

"Though commonly by the trim of a ship is understood the swimming of her, either ahead or astern or on an even keel, in whether of these the ship goes best; in my mind that is not only to be counted her trim, for some ships will go well or ill according to the staying of the masts, the slackness of the shrouds, or the like.

"Therefore the order of her swimming, considered together with this fitting of her masts should be accounted her trim. The way of finding the trim must be in sailing with another ship, by the head so many glasses, by the stern as many, then on an even keel. That way which she goes best is her trim in respect of her mould under water. Then to make her go better, ease the stays or set them up, also the shrouds; then wedge the mast, or give it leave to play; and so in time it is easy (with a little diligence) to find the trim of a ship. Next to Men of War (whose practice daily it is) the Scotsmen are the best in the world to find out the trim of a ship, for they will never be quiet, but try her all ways, and if there be any goodness in her they will make her go."

We need not doubt that a good seaman like Christopher Newport tried the *Susan* all ways and in the end "made her go" on the way to Virginia, and that the early settlers in the Chesapeake had a good grounding in the art of sailing a ship.

"When a mast is very high for the proportion of a ship we say it is a taunt mast. Taunt masts and narrow yards are best to sail by a wind for the sails stand so much the sharper, but yet they do wring a ship's side more than a short mast and a broad yard.

"*Hulling* in foul weather is no more than taking in all the sails and tying down the helm to the lee side of the ship (and so if she be a good conditioned ship she will lie easily under the sea). It is not yet agreed on amongst all seamen whether it is better for a ship to *hull* with her topmasts up or down: the most received opinion is to have them down, in respect that generally they suppose the weight aloft will make her *seel* the more dangerously during a storm. (Seeling is a sudden lying down or tumbling to one side or other in a tempest.) But besides the experience which I have to the contrary, I can give this reason why it is best in a dangerous and desperate storm to hull with the topmasts up. All seamen will confess that the weather seel is the most dangerous seel and therefore must grant that it is the safest hulling which doth most prevent that seel. If her topmasts be down when she seels to leeward, the less weight overhead she hath to hinder her from coming and rolling back over again to windward the faster she will seel over, and the shorter, so that meeting the windward sea so short and suddenly it may endanger to break in and founder her; but if the topmast be up she must needs be the longer in coming up to windward and so meet the sea with more ease that it may have leisure to break away under her; yet it is true she will make the greater lee seel, but in that there is no danger, though to an inexperienced man there may seem to be."

This quotation will set us wondering whether the three little ships which lay ahull away off the Chesapeake on the night of the 21st of April, 1607, had their topmasts up or down. I suspect they were up. Anyway it is quite certain that if the shade of Sir Henry Mainwaring drifts about the waters where race today the little ships with the taunt Bermudian masts, he will approve of them. He will know that they will come slowly to a weather seel and, although he may have some anxiety for the wringing of their sides, he will not be surprised that the high, narrow sail plan makes them fine ships to go by a wind.

Only one more quotation — for what was intended as a footnote grows yards long — that shall be on the still troublesome question of preserving a ship under water. Mainwaring says that:

"Sheathing is done with thin boards, hair, and tar laid betwixt the ship's sides and those boards, the use whereof is to keep the worms from eating through the planks, as generally in all places to the southward they do. The thinner the boards the better, for then will the worm presently be at the tar, which he cannot abide."

Nathaniel Butler, who cribs from Mainwaring all through, to this adds a bit of his own, saying he has been told that red pepper mixed with the tar and pitch will preserve the ship from being eaten by the worm:

"And surely this is not incredible, considering the extreme heat and violent biting nature of this red pepper, which being but tasted gets all the mouth afire."

And this touching picture of the poor worm, coming out of its hole and politely turning its head aside to sneeze, will serve for a tailpiece.

VII

THE MAYFLOWER

THE MAYFLOWER, 1620

THE MAYFLOWER

*How a Chartered Merchantman Helped to Colonize
New England*

THE story of the *Mayflower*, as now commonly accepted, is of a voyage of unparalleled hardship and misery in the company of a rascally captain bribed to land the Pilgrim Fathers in the wrong part of America, where they might be all frozen to death and their splendid adventure brought to nought. This pretty story is put forward in spite of the fact that in the account left us by Governor Bradford, a responsible leader of the Pilgrims, there is no sign of the writer suspecting any double dealing by the captain, nor is there in the earliest printed account by Edward Winslow a sign of suspicion of treachery.

We know how some of the founders wished to try their fortune further on, where they had originally intended, but the majority were for remaining where they had struck the coast; and whatever may be the opinion of Americans generally, Massachusetts folk to a man will resent their State being described as the wrong part of America. To express an opinion on so delicate a matter is quite beyond my book. What does come properly within its covers is the question of the character of the seaman who figures prominently in this first chapter of the history of New England — the master of the *Mayflower*.

It would be difficult to bring a more serious charge against a shipmaster than that of having accepted a bribe to maroon his passengers, yet it has been lightly made by respectable gentlemen whose literary abilities obviously far transcend their knowledge of sea conditions; who, in effect, have hanged the captain of the *Mayflower* high up like a common malefactor, upon evidence insufficient to hang a dog. It is time and overtime these gentlemen were made to cut down the corpse and bury it decently, laying over it a simple stone inscribed "Here lies an Honest Seaman."

Since romantic writers have worked so much embroidery around the story it will be necessary to strip first to the simple facts as they have come down to us.

Unfortunately the captain's account of the voyage is missing, but we may suppose that if that puritanically matter-of-fact weekly, *Lloyds Shipping Index*, had been in circulation in 1620 there would have appeared something to this effect: "*Mayflower*. 180 tons burden, 236 tons gross. Jones, master, left Plymouth, Eng. Sept. 6 with passengers. Arr. Cape Cod, New England. Nov. 9." In the casualty list there might have been added: "Ship arrived leaking badly with damage to upper works, temporarily repaired at sea." That is about all the information Mr. Jones would have given the owners, and I doubt whether he gave

Mrs. Jones and the children much more when he returned home to Rotherhithe.

Governor William Bradford is more communicative. From him we gather that the original intention was to make the passage in two vessels but, the smaller of these springing a leak, both returned. After landing any who did not feel equal to the rough conditions and transferring to the larger ship those who were still determined, final departure was made from Plymouth full late in the year to give hope of a quick passage.

After a spell of fine weather and favorable winds the *Mayflower* met the westerlies; continuous head seas soon began to tell on an old wooden ship and she opened in her upper works, to the great discomfort of her hundred passengers. Then "one of the main beames in the midd ships was bowed and craked . . . the carpenter and master affirmed that with a post put under it set firme in the lower deck and otherwise bounde he would make it sufficiente." Someone thought of using a great iron screw (which the Pilgrims were transporting) as a jack to bring the beam into position, thus lightening the labor. There was a question of turning back but Jones undertook to recaulk the deck and, although he would not promise that her upper works would remain tight, he could promise to get the ship safely across in reasonable comfort if she were not overpressed with sail. It was agreed to carry on. The ship was carefully nursed and we may suppose it was only in the gentlest weather that topsails were set, while in anything approaching a hard wind she laid to and for days together drifted. Her passengers had read in their Bibles how the Lord had broken the ships of Tarshish with an east wind and they must have wondered sometimes whether the Devil were not trying to break their ship with a southwester, as she was lifted up to the heavens and carried down to the depths between the heavy lead-colored seas of the Atlantic.

The younger and more robust Pilgrims we may be sure found some pleasure in the voyage, for the Viking inheritance was theirs and had not entirely disappeared under the weight of the doleful Hebrew view of the sea as reflected in the Old Testament. They heard the master blow his whistle and the boatswain take up the tune with his as he set the mariners to their work; they were fascinated, as intelligent people always are, at the sight of craftsmen who know their trade and practice it well; and had any been so wicked as to have surreptitiously witnessed, before they sailed, Will Shakespeare's new play *The Tempest*, they would have thought, as they heard their own boatswain bawling, that he was the original and that the playwright had drawn him to the life in that opening scene where the stir and breath of a whole howling gale of wind blows right home to the beholder.

And in the calmer intervals youngsters might have been seen learning from old salts to splice a rope, to make bends and hitches, and to know their compass, some even getting on the right side of the one-legged sea cook — happen the other leg had been lost in the Channel in fight against the Spanish Armada. By him they were well stuffed with dough cake as well as with weird and wonderful tales of the sea and, before the voyage was done, those Pilgrim lads were wiser in one respect than old King Solomon in all his wisdom and glory; they at any rate knew something of the way of a ship in the sea, which was more than ever he did to his life's end. I know there is none of this in the Governor's journal and yet you need not doubt that it is all true; there were one-legged sea cooks long before John Silver, and youngsters at sea have been the same in all ages.

For the older and weaker passengers who lay below in the darkness and damp, conditions grew rapidly worse and worse as the voyage was prolonged. The stench of the bilges, of stale food and stale beer, the shortage of fresh water, the horror of rats, who grew more familiar as folk grew more sickly, the closeness of the quarters and the lack of privacy made up a life calling upon all the reserves of their Faith to make it endurable. Sea life for the sickly is indeed no more than imprisonment with the ever present fear of being drowned and we can imagine how these poor souls longed and longed for the shout of "Land ho," particularly Mistress White and Goodwife Allerton who, we know, were both feeling poorly.

Yet it is as well to remember that during the twelve previous years there had been a fairly steady stream of traffic to Virginia, wherein the lot of poor passengers was no less pitiable. There has been a continuous stream since of world migration, and almost to within memory emigrant conditions were little bettered. The case of the early settlers bound for Australia and New Zealand — a voyage of far greater length — must have called for a patience and endurance beyond belief; the case of the African migrations will not bear writing about. Yes, the people in the *Mayflower* suffered, but they did not suffer alone. America is full of the descendants of those who, in ships with names long forgotten, endured as much and more but they, being unblessed with the gift of literary expression, left behind them no word of their sufferings. There are some advantages in being able to spell.

Weeks ran into months and still there was no land. The shortening days meant long anxious nights for the master and, although none of his passengers had died, the sick grew daily weaker, adding greatly to his anxieties. Then, on the sixty-fourth day out, came a sight of the land which the mate recognised as Cape Cod. As the intention was for the Hudson River, the *Mayflower* stood to the southward with a fair wind and in pleasant weather, but soon after noon the wind came dead ahead; shoals with the seas breaking white upon them were sighted. At this pass the captain decided to bear up again for the Cape, where at long last the ship safely anchored as the light flickered — all "happy to get out of those dangers before night overtook them."

Bradford does not question the master's judgment in returning, nor has he a word against him for his conduct of the voyage, but he has a bitter complaint against one of the crew. We had better have it in his own words and spelling: —

"A proud and very profane yonge man, one of the seamen, of a lusty able body which made him the more hauty; he would allway be contemning the poore people in their sickness and cursing them daily with execrations and did not let [fail] to tell them that he hoped to help to caste half of them overboard before they came to their journey's end, and to make mery with what they had; and if he were by any gently reproved, he would curse and swear most bitterly. But it pleased God before they came half seas over to smite this yonge man with a greevous disease of which he died in desparate manner and so was himself the first to be throwne overboard. Thus his curses light on his own head, and it was an astonishment to all his fellows for they noted it to be the just hand of God upon him."

Although we shall never know this husky lad's name I think we can make a shrewd guess at his particular duty, explaining though may be not altogether excusing his profanity. There were in ships of those days two whose special duty it was to keep the ship clean — the Swabber and his mate the Liar. "The swabber," to quote a contemporary writer, "is to keep the cabins and all the rooms of the ship clean within board and the liar to do the like without board. The liar holds his place but for a week and he that is first taken with a lie on a Monday morning is proclaimed at the mainmast with a general cry — 'A liar, a liar!' and for that week he is under the swabber."

In a cargo carrier the duties were not too heavy; in a ship crowded with sadly seasick passengers who did not know the weather side from the lee, conditions must have been enough to try the patience of a saint and we may be sure that he whose appointment dated from Monday would have run out of patience by Tuesday, however long the virtue of his superior office may have lasted. To have been mendacious on Monday morning and to have spent the rest of the week pulling the legs of the poor Pilgrims marks him as a bad lad. Nevertheless capital punishment seems on the border line of severity. After all he was young, and had he lived he might have turned as truthful as George Washington — or very nearly.

There is a general complaint of lack of humanity on the part of the crew while the ship lay in New England, and a specific instance given, where Bradford, who was ill, asked for a can of beer, to be met with answer that "even were my own Father to ask he would be refused." Fairly obviously, I think, here was the steward — the man responsible for seeing that his sea victuals were not depleted against the voyage home — in duty bound refusing the request. Excellent man and learned though he was, the Governor did not realize that away back and beyond Moses and the prophets in whom he was well versed, there lies the Law and Custom of the Sea, based on the grim necessities of the rough and tumble of the sailor's life and the fact that, as old sailors put it, "there is no backdoor to run out of to buy what you want at sea." Preoccupied with thoughts of the great work before him, he never came to know the seamen, or surely he would have forgiven them and hardly have troubled to write down his complaints ten years after the event. This querulousness might be passed over in silence were it not clear indication that, had there been any ground for complaint against the captain, Governor Bradford would have used it.

In the narrative itself there is nothing which might not be expected in a late autumn voyage across the North Atlantic in an old wooden ship. Even as late as the nineteenth century a passage of fifty-three days was not considered out of the way, so that the *Mayflower's* sixty-four days does not disclose a plot to drown Pilgrims. We know she frequently lay to, whereby she would inevitably make much leeway, and, as in October and November the prevailing winds are south-westerly, inevitably she would be set well to the northward. Therefore there was nothing unnatural or suspicious in her landfall at Cape Cod when making for the Hudson — it was, in fact, to be expected. Nevertheless, as Jones had no practical means of ascertaining longitude and on the 9th of November would have had but a hazy idea how far he had fetched to the westward, it is likely that, at the last, the appearance of the Cape a little surprised him. Surely had he lived to hear his landfall described as an act of calculated villainy he would have chuckled; how glad he must have been to get hold of something sure after those many days of uncertainty!

Arrival on the coast threw the main responsibility for the navigation on John Clarke, pilot and mate, and the falling amongst the shoals when the ship stood to the southward must be attributed to his ignorance, bad luck, or malevolence. It would seem unlikely, judging by the time given to a southerly course on that day, that the *Mayflower* ever came in sight of Nantucket shoals, but it is interesting to read in a pilotage book published as late as 1873, that these shoals were "but very little known till within a few years, and then their limits were more exactly defined at the expense of a private individual." The compiler goes on to say that still some doubt exists as to their extent and mentions the discovery of another patch as late as 1860. Such being the case, it is more than reckless to suggest that Clarke or Jones deliberately took a wrong course on the American coast in 1620 so that the Pilgrim Fathers might not reach their desired haven. If in 1873 there was uncertainty as to the extent of so important a danger, how could a poor pilot in the early history of the American coast be expected to have knowledge of the lesser obstructions to navigation?

It amounts to this: there is neither direct accusation of treachery nor a scrap of circumstantial evidence in the account upon which a charge could be maintained. However, in the year 1669, forty-nine years after the event, Nathaniel Morton printed the accusation. A charge made so late in the day might well be treated with suspicion, indeed it always has been so treated by historians of the first rank. Others, without a thought, accepted it as true and then looked round cheerfully for evidence to justify their acceptance. That is their way and in this particular case it landed them with both feet in the mud.

It happens that while both early narratives give the master's name as Jones (Bradford prefers to spell it Joans), neither of them give his christian name and to this omission can be traced most of the trouble; for it happened that in quite early days a certain Captain Thomas Jones appeared on the coast. This fellow was none too good — in fact, a scoundrel. Imaginative historical writers who are ofttimes imaginative only in patches, promptly identified this Jones with Bradford's "Joans" and Winslow's Jones, entirely forgetting the dimensions of the Jones family and the odd chance that more than one member of it may have been foolhardy enough to go to sea. Out of hand these good people appointed Thomas Jones master of the *Mayflower*.

It was useless when a quiet scholar fellow demurred, suggesting that when the *Mayflower* sailed Thomas was elsewhere, and it was hard to see how a man could be in two places at the same time. It was useless when Marsden, a lawyer of international reputation in seafaring matters, exhibited Admiralty Court records showing clearly how the man responsible for the safe conducting of the Pilgrims oversea was christened Christopher. Commercial interest, religious and political prejudice, all combined in demanding a double-dyed villain as captain. In Thomas Jones they possessed one who completely filled the bill, whereas in the case of Christopher the scholars could give no guarantee of ruffianism — for aught they knew to the contrary he might on enquiry turn out to be a saint.

So Christopher Jones' appointment as master of the *Mayflower* has not been confirmed in popular history books, which I think is a pity, for the old prejudices — which kept out reason as an oilskin keeps out rain — are fast dying and there is a growing public which gains as much pleasure from reading truth as it does from reading fiction. Such are likely to be interested in learning how it was that the true name of the famous little ship's captain was put beyond a doubt.

At the time of the Tercentenary Celebrations, the late Dr. Horrocks decided to check over the work of earlier scholars. He determined to search the Customs Books and Port Books of the period which are still preserved. Right away he was faced with a difficulty. Instead of one *Mayflower* he found a whole bunch. His first task was to pick out one labelled "Jones, master."

He found that in August, 1609, a ship called *Mayflower* cleared the Port of London for Drontheim in Norway, her cargo consisting of hats, hemp, Spanish salt, hops and Gascon wine; bringing home tar, deals and good red herring. Her master's name was Christopher Jones and he is also given as part owner. The ship was followed in the old ledgers trading to La Rochelle or Bordeaux, always Christopher Jones, Master, and carrying principally cottons, bays, buffins, says and fustians, varied with rabbit skins, iron stubs and stockings — all these outward. Homeward she brought sometimes salt, more often Cognac and Gascony wine. It was such a cargo that Christopher Jones discharged in May, 1620. No entries were to be found in the second half of that year and none in the first half of 1621. Then — "October 31st *Mayflower*, Christopher Jones, Master, salt from La Rochelle."

Dates are a nuisance but we must recall that in July, 1620, two months after Jones discharged a cargo of wine, a ship called *Mayflower* was chartered for a voyage to New England. She sailed in September to arrive in November and on the 5th of April she left that happy land to arrive in the Old Country on May 6th. There is, of course, nothing mysterious about her absence from the Customs Registers in the intervening time, for there was no export duty on Pilgrim Fathers and there was nought to pay on an empty ship.

Beyond any reasonable doubt, then, the ship loading for Norway in 1609 and the ship crossing the Atlantic with the founders of New England eleven years afterwards were one and the same. Nor can we doubt that he who commanded in 1609 was he who sang out "Stand clear o' the cable" and "Let go!" as the weather-beaten little ship lost way under Cape Cod on the evening of the 9th of November, 1620 — by name, Christopher Jones.

The entry of October 31st, 1621, in the Customs book is the last wherein master and ship are associated. The master was growing old. In the register of St. Mary Rotherhithe is to be found: "Christopher Jones buried March 5th, 1622."

That was his end; of his beginning little is known. At one time he lived in Harwich, but for the last eleven years of his life he made a home for his family at Rotherhithe. It seems probable that some time he went awhaling, and it is certain that, at the time of the Atlantic voyage, he had behind him a record of fourteen years as master with the same firm, first in the *Josan* then for twelve years in the *Mayflower*, and of her we know he was part owner. Having been so long in one employment in a regular trade, we may fairly assume he held a reputation for shrewdness and honesty — the last sort of a man a rogue would risk approaching with a bribe. Rogues know that seamen of that rough-hewn type are likely to tell them to go to Hell and take their money with them.

But a public so lavishly fed upon a sea literature all bloodstained belaying pins, bullying and blasphemy, has gotten firmly into mind that in the days of sail the trade of the world was always carried on to such an accompaniment; consequently, with no evidence to the contrary, they are liable to assume every seaman a ruffian. It is a false picture. I do not mean that in the majority of ships the language spoken came up to the high standard of the Sunday school, but I do mean that the sailing ship masters, to whom we are but now waving farewell, were in the main, normal, decent human beings — the abnormal brute commanding a shipload of vice and misery being the rare exception.

Bearing this in mind and remembering that sailors do not change much, the chances are that the master of the *Mayflower* was an honest seaman.

Nathaniel Morton's accusation against Christopher Jones therefore stands isolated and without documentary support. We know that, as he wrote his *New England's Memorial*, he held the Governor's journal in his hand and we know that there he found no warrant for his charge. But he wrote at a time in the history of the country when people believed firmly that they were of the Elect. Inevitably such folk are ever slow to recognise virtue and quick to discover vice in any outside their own creed. Bradford's omission of any word of thanks to Christopher for his care in bringing the Pilgrims safely through the perils of the sea was as a vacant plot wherein to grow suspicion, and in suitable climate this flowered into definite assertion of evil. By that time the old sailor had long lain under the turf and there was none left to say a word for him.

But if people had turned back to the earliest printed account of the voyage they would have found that one of the Fathers at least had some regard and felt some gratitude. Edward Winslow has left a picture of Christopher — no more than a miniature to fit a locket. A memory of him ashore walking up and down in the snow with the Pilgrims, and at eventide carrying the weaker on board his ship to save them from the bitterness of the night.

Christopher Columbus of the *Santa Maria*, Christopher Newport of the *Susan Constant*, and Christopher Jones of the *Mayflower*, were three noted ferrymen of the Atlantic. Some will know that Christopher is a happy name for a ferryman.

The "Mayflower" lying to under mizzen

VIII

THE ROYAL SOVEREIGN

THE ROYAL SOVEREIGN, 1637

THE ROYAL SOVEREIGN

Phineas Pett's Greatest Ship and England's Bid
for Sea Power

IN THE HOLD of a half-built ship stood the ever kingly figure of Charles the
First, and beside him was a crafty looking elderly man who was reckoned the
best shipwright in England. And here — the air filled with the scent of freshly
hewn timber — the King first made known to Phineas Pett his resolve to build a
new ship, to be the greatest in the world, of 1500 tons and to carry one hundred
and two bright brass guns. It was a great moment, for it was England's first claim
to supremacy at sea; and it was a tragic moment, for it was the demand for money
to build the great ship which brought the crowd against the King — the first step
in the royal progress which was to end one bitter winter's morning in 1649 on the
scaffold at Whitehall. But on that bright summer's morning at Woolwich in 1634,
there were no clouds, no evil portents. All seemed well for the King, standing in the
hold of the *Leopard* building for his Navy Royal.

Now it was all very well for Charles in his regal way to write down 1500 tons
and 102 guns, but it left old Phineas with a pretty stiff problem to face. He could
manage the tonnage all right — just fiddle with the figures a bit and make her of
as many tons as he liked. The cannon, however, of which he was given the weight,
were a different matter. There was the powder and shot — and a great deal of
that might be blazed away in a single action. Then there was the crew; in those
days a ship had to carry six months' provisions for her men. Phineas reckoned that
seven hundred seafaring folk would eat a power of salt pork, yellow peas, and hard
bread in that time, and the beer for those seven hundred thirsty seamen — barrels
and barrels and barrels! Small wonder these old ships were bulky, bulgy looking
old busses. For all that, the best of them had a fine run aft so that the water came
clean to the rudder.

Phineas plucked at his beard, bit the butt end of his pen and laid down lines
of the best on his board, then set his son Peter to make the model with three flush
decks armed all along with cannon, a patter which was to stand for all great ships
for over two centuries.

But early in the game there was a cry of check. The Elder Brethren of Trinity
House, who in those days had a word to say on all seafaring matters, solemnly decided that it was beyond the wit of man to devise a serviceable vessel with three
flush decks armed; and, if she were built, there was nowhere (except the Wight)
where she could be havened; no anchors which could hold her, and if there were,
and those anchors were down (said they) no crew could ever get them up again.

[69]

These particular elder brothers belonged to a much larger order which is world wide and has existed in all ages — the Order of St. Precedent, whose rule is ever to look backwards, whose gospel is: "That which never has been, can never be."

But the King took not the slightest notice of their petition, the preparations for the building of the ship swept along and, by the summer following, the diocese of the Bishop of Durham was invaded by a whole army of shipwrights who spread themselves through the leafy woods, carrying their moulds and patterns with them to ensure that the right shaped timber might be harvested for her curving frames and crooked knees. Phineas and son Peter came up by ship to Newcastle and soon the bishop was moving, the knights of the county were moving and, willy nilly, the country folk — mere pawns in the game — were lending a hand. It was a great labor, for that summer two thousand five hundred great oaks were "felled, hove and haulded" to the waiting Castle ships in the Tyne. Twenty-four oxen and four strong horses had their work cut out to drag one giant, which was for the keelson, down the dale to the waiting Castle ship and it took a great deal of heaving and sweating and cursing to get him aboard, we may be sure of that. But it was pleasant enough in the green wood when the sawing and felling was done for the day. They brewed good ale in Durham.

Phineas stayed but to see a good beginning and then made tracks for home, riding through the heart of England, seeing in his mind's eye great and yet greater ships where other men saw only trees. At Huntingdon, he turned off the main road towards Cambridge. Much water had passed down the Cam since he was last beside it.

Phineas Pett came of a family of shipwrights. He was fifth in a direct line and could scarcely count the uncles and cousins who practised the Art. As a small boy at Deptford, he had romped with his brothers and sisters in the chips and shavings which came from the famous *Revenge*, and he had watched his father build the *Rainbow* and many other famous ships. In 1586, however, he had turned away from all that — gone up to Cambridge. When, one night two years later, the beacons burnt bright throughout England and *Rainbow*, *Revenge* and the rest were biting the heels of the tall Spaniards in the Channel, young Phineas was to be found bent over his book, a scholar at Emmanuel, dreaming perhaps that one day he might become Dean of St. Paul's or even Archbishop of Canterbury, who knows?

Then his father died; supplies were cut off — those dreams were ended. He turned again to the shipyard to find his brothers, who had stuck to their trade, showing a hard face towards him. He became a poor apprentice, so poor that after two years this Bachelor of Arts of Cambridge University was glad to ship as carpenter's mate of a privateer working the Levant and the coast of Barbary, where they took many hazards but few prizes. Returning as poor as when he went away, he was glad for a long time to work as an ordinary hand in the yards. But slowly he pushed his way through and upwards and, at the end of twenty years, Phineas Pett found himself building the *Prince Royal* for King James I. She was the great ship of her day. Now, in his old age, he had designed the last word in the wooden ship of war and was come back to his old University as the Master of Ship-wrightry. It must have been a great day for him, that 31st of July, 1635, at Cambridge, but he wrote no more in his diary than that he lodged at the Falcon, visited his old College and went his way homeward.

By Christmastide the last of the laden Castle ships had come into Woolwich Reach. The ground ways were prepared and the keel was laid on the splitting blocks: stem and sternpost were raised, frames were set up; keelson, clamps, wales and beams were bolted and bound together to the incidental music of a shipyard which is written for adze, saw, big hammer, little hammer, mallet, maul and beetle. Meanwhile the Elder Brethren stood shaking their grey beards and still droning their dismal prophesies of disaster to so great a ship. But Peter, who conducted the orchestra, and Phineas, who had written the score, had ears only for their own music. The frame finished, they started to plank up the vessel; the blue smoke ascended from the boiling pitch and the caulkers rang their mallets. The time was drawing near when she would become a Sea Worthy.

While the carpenters pressed on with the serious building, the painters and carvers were preparing the adornments. Besides the statue of King Edgar ahorse,

STARBOARD TACK ~ THE OLD WAY ~ LARBOARD TACK

trampling on seven kings, which was to beautify the head, the designer, being something of a classical scholar, furnished her stern with a surprisingly large selection from the heathen mythology while roses, crowns, harps and thistles, with all the signs of the zodiac, decorated her sides, interspersed with several Latin mottoes. These last were to be to the after confounding of many a hardy old tarpaulin commander and there was a great deal of boggling, too, over the names of the heroes of antiquity.

The Navy never did quite understand what it was all about, but they thought it looked pretty and were annoyed when a cannon shot knocked Edgar off his horse and powder and smoke changed the color of Aeolus's chameleon. These little tragedies were to happen many years after in battle with the Dutch. Meanwhile in Woolwich Yard gaping apprentices stood lost in wonderment at the skill of the carvers and painters, and doubtless many drab little houses in Woolwich were brightened with crude copies of the signs and wonders which adorned King Charles's noble three-decker.

From the time of the laying of the keel to the day when all the shipwrights of the River were called together to strike her onto the ways, it was nearly two years. On the day appointed by the king for her launching, the tide gave short measure, the great ship stuck and neither the boatswain's blasphemies — and he gave full measure — nor the yo-hoing and heaving on the tackles by all the King's men would budge her one inch. So disconsolate King, Queen, lords and ladies trooped back to the palace again, the ceremony perforce postponed till next spring tides. On the night before the newly appointed day, coming a hot tide, the ship was found to be afloat and Phineas, who was getting very bored with the Elders (they having redoubled their croakings since the first failure to launch), decided to risk the royal displeasure, dispense with ceremony and haul her off to her moorings. In the morning, for all the world to see, there she was in her own element at last — the finest ship in Christendom, the *Sovereign of the Seas*.

The ship being afloat, they stepped masts and rigged her with a main yard 103½ feet long, a mizzenyard of 81 feet and the spritsail yard on her bowsprit, 63 feet. She crossed royal yards over her topgallants on her fore and main with a topgallant yard on her mizzen. They gave her four twenty-inch cables of hemp and four more of nineteen inches and it is not reported that her crew ever had any difficulty in getting her anchors. It is amusing to find that this great ship, of which were prophesied so many evil things because she was so great, measured just about 172½ feet between perpendiculars with a beam of 48 feet. But to those who gazed on her when she was completed for sea in 1638, who saw her wreathed in the smoke of the 72 gun salute which she gave when the King made his final inspection she seemed great enough. Well might old Phineas Pett reckon that he and his son Peter had produced a very pretty ship to set before the King.

Through the troubled waters of internal political strife the *Sovereign* carried her way. Charles I came to journey's end; Cromwell came, stood and passed; Charles II came to his own again and left it with a jest; and when James II made way for King William to enter, the old ship was afloat and ready for service. Her name had been altered to *Royal Sovereign*, her wings had been clipped long since, her spar decks had been swept away and where King Edgar once rode was the image of a lion, rampant and roaring. But throughout her many repairings and rebuildings she retained the principal dimensions and the sweep and rhythm of the lines as they had been laid down on her designer's board in 1634.

Before she went up in a sheet of flame in 1696, the *Royal Sovereign* had won a proud record in the line of battle. In her first fight off the Kentish Knock in 1652, it was reported in a letter from the fleet that "that great ship, a delicate frigate (I think the whole world hath not her like) did her part: she sailed through and through the Hollanders and played hard upon them. And at one time there were about twenty Hollander frigates upon her, but blessed be the Lord she hath sustained no very great loss." On St. James's Day in '66 she was next astern of the Commander-in-Chief flying a "blodied" broad pennant and commanded by the valiant Captain John Cox. It was he who, as master of the flagship, had refused to shorten sail when in chase on the night of the Battle of Lowestoft.

At Solebay in '72, old Sir Joseph Jordan, a veteran of sixty-nine, slashed her through the Dutch center. At Texel Fight in '73, she flew the flag of Prince Rupert. There she lost her captain, gallant Sir Wiliam Reeves. Again, at Beachy Head, she flew the flag of the Commander-in-Chief and finally, at the great victory of Barfleur in 1692, at her foretopmast head was the flag of Sir Ralph Delaval, Vice Admiral of the Red.

Throughout her long life the men who served in the *Royal Sovereign* spoke well of her. Prince Rupert told King Charles II that she was the finest ship he had "riding or sailing." Once, meeting a head wind when coming into the Thames, Rupert tacked the great ship right through the narrows. As she stirred the mud with her heel and went shooting into the wind with blocks banging and canvas slatting and thundering, the one-time cavalryman turned to Phineas Pett's grandson, who was beside him, and with a laugh shouted, "And what do you think Trinity House would say to this?"

NOTE ON THE PLAN OF THE "SOVEREIGN OF THE SEAS"

No contemporary plans or models of the *Sovereign* exist. It has been proved that those plans which have been published date from 1817 and are incorrect in some particulars. The dimensions of the ship which are known are:

Length: Keel, 127′; with false post, 128′. Between perpendiculars, 172′. Gun deck, 167′ 9″. Over all, 232′.

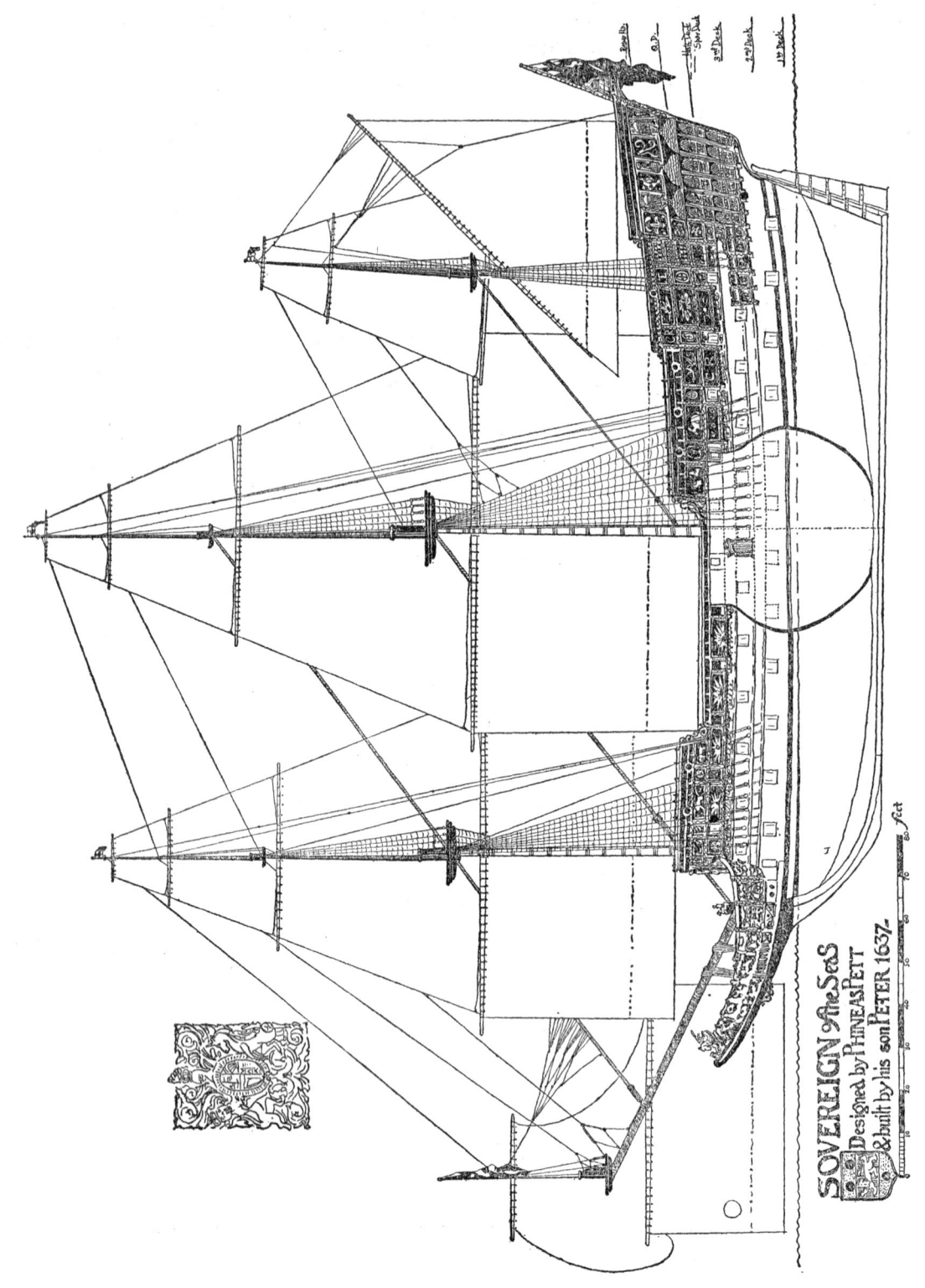

SOVEREIGN of the SeaS
Designed by PhineasPett
& built by his son Peter 1637.

Breadth: Moulded, 46′ 6″. Outside plank 48′ 0½″.

Depth: In hold, 18′ 4″. External, 19′ 6″.

Height: Between decks, 7′ 6″ or 7′ 3″. From keel to top of poop lanter, 76′. The height of her lower deck ports from the water was designed to be 4′ 6″ but she came below her marks.

There are complete measurements of her masts, spars, and sails and there are data on which her midship section and rising line can be plotted. The accompanying plan has been constructed on these particulars and can therefore be taken as a near approximation to the drawing on Phineas Pett's board in 1635. The only important particulars missing are the stations of her masts; these have been stepped in positions usual at the time. The general layout of the decorations is from a contemporary drawing in the possession of Mr. Junius Morgan. As designed, she was found crank and in 1651 her upper works were cut down six feet.

The only rigging shown in the plan are stays, shrouds, and backstays. The sails are shown with bonnets laced.

IX
THE ANDREW

THE ANDREW, 1652

THE ANDREW

*The Story of an American Who Commanded Cromwell's
Blockading Squadron*

A LITTLE short of three hundred years ago there came from Wapping to Massachusetts a ship's carpenter rejoicing soberly in the name of Nehemiah Bourne. Now in those days the title of ship's carpenter might mean what it means today or it might mean more, for when metacenters and such like were unheard of, theory and practice were on better terms, and the man who designed a ship often built and even had the courage to go to sea in her. Nehemiah was of this sort — hopeful designer, skillful carpenter and bold mariner. In the light of after events, it would seem probable that political and religious differences in the old country brought him to try his fortune in the new one; it is hardly likely to have been financial trouble, for with him industry was backed by remarkable business capacity.

Marrying not long after his arrival, in 1640, he and his wife, Hannah, were blessed with a son, so that he seemed securely moored in his new home. But when trouble broke out in England between Charles I and his Parliament, Nehemiah buckled on a sword and, recrossing the Atlantic, joined the Parliamentary Army, finding himself by 1644 a major in Rainsborough's famous regiment. He did not remain long in the army. Always claiming to be a peaceful business man, as soon as the issue of the Civil War was put beyond doubt, Bourne returned to his trade.

In 1650 we hear of him again; this time in command of one of his own ships, resisting an attack by two Dutch privateers who found in the peaceful merchantman commanded by a pacifist something of a surprise packet — they thought themselves lucky to get away with burnt fingers. It happened that at this time Cromwell, who was building a fine fleet of ships, was looking for men to command them. He remembered Major Bourne's soldiering days and suggested that an attempt be made to wean him from his mercantile pursuits so that he might serve in the navy, and not long afterwards he appears as commander-in-chief of the blockading squadron off the coast of Scotland. Blockade is unpicturesque work, but if it is thorough enough it nullifies the most brilliant action ashore; it was in 1651, and Scotland lost. The Massachusetts man had found a new career.

From now on he comes more into the limelight and we see him in detail — in more detail than most men of action, because, besides having learned to handle chisel, hammer and sword, he had acquired facility with the pen, and after a hard day's work he seems to have found no difficulty in sitting down to write a detailed report of his doings. These reports have been preserved; they are long-winded, they wander off into personal matters but they wander back again, and by the time he has subscribed himself somebody's "very humble and ready servant" we have a clear idea of the day's work and we know something more of Nehemiah. Certainly he was never terse, and I suspect that is one reason why he has never become a popular hero, for the naval heroes chiefly beloved of writers usually write tersely. To be sure, a deal of time must have been wasted in times past composing terse reports on muddled and desultory actions. However, circumlocutory in correspondence he might be, Bourne was always abrupt in action.

On May 18th, 1652, he was lying in the Downs wearing a flag at the maintopmast head of the *Andrew*, with eight other ships under his command. Robert Blake was twenty miles SW with the main fleet. The wind was NE and it was hazy. War had not been declared with Holland, though relations were hanging on a strand. At ten o'clock, through the haze, Bourne saw a Dutch fleet of forty-one sail passing down on the back side of the Goodwin Sands. A small ketch was hailed and ordered to clap on all sail and she was soon tearing down wind to warn Blake while Nehemiah wondered what next. He saw the big fleet lie to off the South Sand head, while two frigates stood for the Downs. The *Greyhound* was sent out to demand their business. They came in to say, with Admiral Tromp's respects, that their fleet came for shelter, for which reason they were on their way to anchorage in Dover Bay. The Dutch captains reported afterwards to Tromp that the Admiral in the Downs had been very pleasant with them, but he had finished the conversation by saying that he would better believe their reason for coming when they had cleared out again. He also told them that whether they intended war or peace did not signify much to him, but he "wished the hand of God might be on the man who should be the first cause of a breach." The Dutchmen would have noticed he was cleared for action and had his cable hove short. That night he had two of his frigates stationed with a code of signals to indicate any movements, and of course a letter went post haste to London, with apologies for its brevity, explaining it was as full as "time and other business would admit." It had been a trying day and doubtless Nehemiah turned in early.

In the morning came a message from Blake; he was coming, turning up over a fair tide along the shore, and about the same time Tromp was seen getting under way and standing towards Calais. There was no hurry. Half Channel over, the big fleet was seen to fling round and stand towards Blake; there was hustle in the Downs. As Bourne came clear of the South Foreland he could see battle smoke ahead and his ships were soon a smother of canvas. To Blake, who was being badly mauled, their approach seemed slow — the Dutch thought it quick enough. Blake was hard pressed until the carpenter-admiral's squadron fell like a hammer on Tromp's rear and smashed it. Tromp hauled off, leaving two fragments of his fleet with the English.

In such manner began the first Dutch war. Blake and Tromp were both honest men but they could never agree as to who fired the first broadside. Nehemiah had no doubts; the hand of the Lord was on the Dutch; thenceforward the man worked and fought as one inspired.

But so far as actual fighting was concerned he was to take part in only one more battle. In September he was again lying in the Downs, Rear Admiral of the Blue, with Blake still Commander-in-Chief and William Penn as Vice-Admiral. The Dutch had been sighted to the NE. Blake and Penn were away early but the Rear Admiral was held up. The accounts of the battle which followed are confusing and contradictory, and difficult to reconstruct, but it would appear that when first sighted the Dutch were lying to close under the lee of the shoal off the Thames Estuary known as the Kentish Knock, the wind being westerly. At the approach of Blake and Penn on the starboard tack, the Dutch filled on the port tack. The English, determined to keep the weather berth, were pinched for room and in effect were luffed on to the obstruction. Blake with his squadron bumped on and off, firing furiously as they passed to the north. Penn was not so fortunate and remained fast for some time, while Bourne was isolated to the south. Tactically, it would appear that Admiral de With had the best of it; but the tide was rising

The "Andrew"

and as Penn came clear he came on the same tack as the Dutch with his head southerly. As in Dover Strait Nehemiah had driven through the enemy rear, so now he came slashing through their van, and all was confusion. By nightfall both fleets were fought to a standstill and in the morning de With reluctantly refused battle. Some of his people had not behaved too well, and several had left in the night.

As was usual, both fleets were badly shattered, the old *Andrew* particularly being in a bad way. The scene of action was shifted for a while to the dockyards in England and Holland, where the thunder of hammers succeeded the thunder of guns, where sailmakers stitched and stitched all day, and in spare moments carpenters made wooden legs for poor maimed sailors to go upon.

It was while the *Andrew* was repairing that Tromp and Blake fell foul again and the English fleet met with disaster, losing two ships. There was misconduct afloat, induced by bad management ashore. At this juncture a new post was found for Nehemiah Bourne.

It is always difficult for people who are out of the smoke and sweat and wet to acquire a sense of the realities of war at sea. It is not often that men don't care about the people afloat — such are generally found out and dealt with — the trouble is with the men who don't know. It was a happy day therefore for the fleet when they heard that Nehemiah was going to take a shore billet, for he was a man who cared, who knew what was wanted and who had the technical skill to ensure that the work was well done. . . . He would have had no illusions about a peaceful life. He had won a reputation as a hard fighting seaman, had this carpenter-admiral, and knew he was coming ashore to fight against ignorance, slackness and graft, just exchanging the fighting *Andrew* for a fighting stone-wall frigate. Nominally, one of eight Navy Commissioners whose duty was the supply of men and material without meddling with strategy, Bourne had some powers in this respect, besides being frequently called upon to advise the Council of State.

His duties began on January 1st, 1653, and needless to say he was at the office early and stayed late, for there was much business on hand. Tromp was known to be away south, preparing to escort a valuable convoy through the English Channel to Holland and preparations were being made to intercept him. Although ships were ready in fair number, there was a shortage of men in the fleet, for smart seamen preferred to sail in privateers where discipline was easier and prize money more plentiful, and the men who were being collected by hundreds in London were bolting while being conveyed to the ports. The need was great. Nehemiah was ordered to bear a hand and his letters written during ten critical days in February give a clear idea of his method of obtaining reinforcements for the fleet; they show him, too, as carpenter, intelligence officer, and strategist.

The first letter from Gravesend is dated February 15th, written at ten o'clock at night by the light of a guttering candle. From it we learn that in the day he had been at dockside in London beating up men. There he had seen some of the *Centurion's* people who should have been on board their ship. They were insolent to him, "which I was forced to endure" — one may guess Nehemiah was a man of small stature. He determines to rope them in later. Before leaving he packs twenty-three men off, on his way down river collecting more. The afternoon is spent selecting the most serviceable ships and pushing them out to sea. He notes a privateer lying in the river and knows better than to board her, reckoning to get most of her crowd ashore that night carousing. From the next letter, dated the 16th, we learn that he turned the mayor and the constable out at four in the morning to comb the town for sailors, and quite early sends fifty away; then afloat driving dilatory captains and helping those who were eager to get into action, sending boats searching miles up river. He works on right through the bitter night, boarding and searching everything that comes down on the ebb, netting hundreds before he returns to the office in the morning. Here he found rumors of battle buzzing in every hour. Then, late on the 19th, a horseman draws rein at the door with news of a fight the day before, beginning by Portland Bill and moving off up Channel. Nehemiah put the lid on his inkpot and prepared to go a journey.

Early the next morning he is as far as Gravesend and is soon galloping towards Rochester. Here he descends like a thunderclap on the naval store officer, waking him up to the fact that there is a war on and demanding all the spare spars in the depot; then on through Kent, slowing to a trot, a crawl, a stop at Canterbury. He can go no further that night "by reason of a great distemper upon me" which apparently was his name for a paralyzing nervous headache. Perhaps the frantic appeal for stores from the storekeeper at Rochester had been met by a request to be shown before delivery the proper forms — "Demand Notes in quadruplicate" maybe — and that had been too much for Nehemiah on a war horse. Anyway, he is physically "beat" for the moment but has strength to send a messenger helter skelter to the Governor of Dover Castle with orders to push out everything that could fight, and advises the government to keep all slow ships safe in the river, sending only the nimble to sea till it is sure that the Dutch are beaten. Doubtless, he had anticipated this latter order in the morning at Gravesend, for that was his little way — do it and ask afterwards.

The next day the dust is seen flying on the road that leads down between the white cliffs into Dover, and out of the cloud emerges Nehemiah, refreshed and ready to take charge of everything and everybody. Prizes and damaged ships are already tumbling in from the sea with muddled accounts as to where the fleets are and how the fight is, all unreliable, as is usual with the stories of those who have been in the thick of it. Out go fast frigates to find the true state of affairs.

For him, days and nights are all run together — Tuesday may be Wednesday or even Thursday — he is picking out ships that can be quickly repaired, putting men on the job and pushing the ships out again, while the hopelessly shattered, with their mangled men still aboard, are pushed aside on to the mud after any serviceable guns have been shifted into likely merchantmen — these go forth to look for Dutch stragglers. At a rumor of a fresh Dutch fleet out, a frigate goes flying to warn a weak English squadron to the north. All the time prizes are coming, some with queer names which Nehemiah doesn't always get quite right — the *Black Buss, Church of Saerdam, Black Raven, George of Medemblick, Princess of Rotterdam, Black Elephant,* the *Church of Graveling* and the *Morning Star.* Vinegar, tobacco, wine, salt, cochineal, prunes, strum and sugar, a wonderful mixture, all consigned to Amsterdam but now in process of being labeled London. Though there is not much doubt now how the day has gone, reinforcements still go out. There is no room for able ships in Dover Harbor where Nehemiah now reigns. Ships were not built to hold up dock walls; "the proper place for a ship is the sea and out you go," was his order.

On the evening of the 22nd, the *Fairfax* with Vice Admiral Lawson's flag flying limps into the road; the admiral is asking for advice as to where he is to go, being in a bad way. It is morning before Nehemiah can get aboard to find that fine ship in a sorry mess, one hundred killed and wounded, her topsides pretty well blown in, cordage mere junk and sails ready for the rag merchant. With craftsman's eye he sees at once that there is scarce a spar that can be made to stand up to its work. "Best get up by Chatham Church," he says, "we can do nothing for you here and like enough they are too busy already at Portsmouth."

With what the Vice Admiral tells him and the information the frigates bring in, he is able to write an appreciation for the Council of State: "I am clear of the opinion that all the Dutch that are not taken or spoiled are got home or very near it." There is time now to cast a compassionate eye on the wounded and prisoners; time to write a postscript to his report, just — "I am quite weary."

On the 24th, in the morning, he sees something which enrages him. A Dutch man-of-war which had been riding outside is being brought in and he notices that she has "not one hawser to warp her into the pier, all had been *imbezold* out in the road before." He had been conscious of this game going on ever since he had been in Dover, but there had been no time to stop it. Sails, gear and provisions out of the prizes were being sold at cut throat prices for the benefit of the small prize crews and their friends ashore, while the seamen still facing it out at sea were being swindled of their dues. This clear instance stirs him to action, tired as he is. He calls on the Mayor for assistance and he calls on the Governor of the Castle, and with this help, civil and military, he rakes right through the town, gathering coils of rope, yards of sail cloth, casks of beer, gallons of Hollands gin and brandy-wine, returning all to the prize officers and daring them to let so much as an ounce of pepper out of their hands without warrant — all to the amazement and disgust of the land sharks. Then Nehemiah, the just, takes up his pen and asks the Admiralty to back his action with their authority. Generally, he was obsequious when writing to his superiors, but in this letter he is almost truculent, and as one reads the opening of his final paragraph — "I have one word more to offer to your Honours" — one can picture him fairly shaking with outraged justice. When he left the fleet at sea, sailors knew that Nehemiah Bourne would stand by them; he never let them down.

Two more days were spent in clearing up operations, and we may be sure that if any Dutch straggler got safe to port it was not Bourne's fault. What could be done had been done for the wounded; masts and stores had been forwarded to Portsmouth, where unexpectedly most of the battered fleet had returned. Then, having set all in order, Nehemiah went up the hill which leads towards London. As he disappeared the rushing wind which had seemed to be blowing since his advent died down, fat officials mopped their brows, took a breather and cursed him for a holy terror.

The next day the little man arrived at the Admiralty, red-nosed and pinched with the cold, for it was February and the wind was in the north. He gave his views, doubtless, about dockyardmen and storekeepers in general, and spoke with asperity in particular of prize masters and prize crews. He presented his account of personal expenses, which was lengthy but just to the last penny. Then we may suppose he retired quietly home to endure another of his "great distempers," soothed by his beloved Hannah.

And that was the man's way throughout the war. The port of Harwich became, naturally, the advance base; here the flotsam of battle drifted — wounded, prisoners, and battered ships — while through it passed orders, dispatches and intelligence, and here Nehemiah settled himself, taking complete control. He found the taverns breeding places of loose talk and mutiny; he closed them. He made a dockyard out of nothing, he boarded out the wounded in the healthier part of the countryside, he begged the Admiralty to obtain a troop of horse to keep order in the town "for the honour of the service," and when they refused, he wrote "two lines" to the Lord General Cromwell. George Monck, the Commander-in-Chief at sea, wrote from the "*Resolution* about three leagues to the south'ard of the Texel" that it was strange to him that twenty ships should be so long in fitting out at the three properly equipped ports whereas Major Bourne had sent twenty-two in half the time from his makeshift dockyard. The man at the front is the best judge of the work of the man at the base, and the many rubs which Nehemiah received from London were soothed by this one word of praise from the sea.

Since he was a family man, it would be ungracious to leave out mention of the family. When Nehemiah came ashore, brother John was made Rear Admiral of the Blue and at the battle of Portland he fought desperately. It was about the time that the elder brother was routing out ill-gotten stores at Dover that he was handed a letter: "Sir, I suppose you have a more full relation of the event of our fleet's engagement than I am able to give you, only you may please to take notice that the *Assistance,* whereof your brother is commander, is come hither, being much torn, in which engagement Providence has so ordered that your brother hath received some wound in his head, but I hope not mortal. I rest your assured loving friend, Francis Willoughby." Major Willoughby's hope was fulfilled. John recovered, spending his convalescence with bandages around his head serving as Flag Captain to Monck, in the two fierce battles which settled the business for the time between England and Holland. Sister Ellen married brave Anthony Earning who was captain of the *Reformation* throughout most of the war, to fall many years afterwards when commanding an Indiaman in action with a Dutch squadron. Their daughter Martha married Admiral Sir Charles Wager, who in the early eighteenth century was to become First Lord of the Admiralty. The girls couldn't go to sea, so they did the next best thing — they married seamen. A great sailor family were the Bournes.

There is no record of Nehemiah serving after the Restoration. His views, both religious and political, were too rooted to fit the new order, yet we know he was one of those who signed a petition against religious persecution in New England and, although we may suppose he put not his trust in princes, he lived quietly enough under Charles II, minding his own business. We know that in 1684 he buried his beloved Hannah in London, but of the date of his own death there is no record. His particular political views had gone out of fashion in England, and in the New World youth had lost all interest in the doings of the Old.

He went unsung, yet songs have been made about many warriors with far less fighting spirit than this plain fellow in high steeple hat, square white collar and black coat, who flew his flag in the *Andrew* in 1652; one suspects that even in those days the head of a carpenter's rule was peeping out of his pocket. Equestrian statues have been raised to the memory of men who were mere tailors' dummies compared with this slip of a man who, one time, might have been seen on a large horse galloping along the lanes which lead to the eastern ports of England, charging into sleepy shipyards, urging and driving men to work — work which he knew must be done if his side were to win.

Nothing material of him remains save a few sheets of paper covered with a faded scrawl, but in the shipyards of Massachusetts today, when a good bit of work is produced, it owes something to the tradition for fine craftsmanship left behind by this early shipbuilder of America; and in the Royal Navy today, that which is done "for the sake of the Service" without a thought of the New Year's Honours List, owes not a little to the tradition handed on by this Rear Admiral of the Blue, who long years ago rejoiced soberly in the name of Nehemiah Bourne.

X

THE ROYAL CHARLES

THE ROYAL CHARLES, 1650

THE ROYAL CHARLES

*How the Father of Pennsylvania's Peace-Loving Quaker
Made Naval History*

EARLY surroundings generally grow up with a man and are entwined into his life; more rarely he mounts a high horse and tramples early environment out of recognition. William Penn of Pennsylvania rode a very high horse and trampled upon his past as St. George tramples upon his dragon; for the constructive and peace loving Quaker had been brought up in times of war and destruction with the usual frivolous reactions and to write his father's story is to write the naval history of the period. Wherever there was fighting at sea, there was to be found Admiral Sir William Penn.

Unlike his superiors, Monk, Blake and Deane who first won laurels on land, Penn was first and last a seaman. These soldier admirals were large minded enough to realize their own shortcomings and appreciate their vice admiral's professional abilities, seeing in him an example of what the naval officer should be; while he, a well educated man, was able to recognize the feeling for better order and closer control in battle brought by them from the "New Model" Army to the service of the sea. He became both an example and an advocate for a new type of naval officer.

It was a time when it was realized that the days of chivalry were done. No longer were groups of ships looked upon as so many squadrons of charging horses, each group independent and serving as a background before which some hereditary heaven-born hero might display his valor as he charged pell mell into the enemy. The thunder of the guns had drowned the sound of the trumpets, the banners emblazoned with a variety of ornate devices had given place to the simple white, red and blue flags of the van, center and rear of a fleet drawn up in a single line, the leaders falling in and blazing away with the rest — leadership shedding much of the pomp and vanity of war to take on the more sober garments of a controlling mind at the center.

In old days soldiers had commanded fleets in the Mediterranean where the man-of-war was the oar-propelled galley with her main battery mounted in the bow. She was a vessel able to turn almost as freely on the sea as a man turns on the barrack square; a fleet of them nigh as easy to maneuver as an army on a plain. When the scene shifted to the ocean, the sailing vessel, with her battery on her broadside, was found infinitely more powerful and efficient than the galley. Henceforth the soldier wishing to command successfully at sea had to come to an understanding of sailor ways.

[89]

In 1652, when the grim faced Puritans and the square faced Dutchmen looked at one another through their gun ports, there were no illusions, each had practiced the new tactics on Spain, both had realized that wind was the power and each strove to gain it in the opening stages of the battle.

The term "getting to windward" of another, meaning to get the better of a man, has long passed into common speech; those who know anything of yacht racing know the importance of the reality. Picture two fleets, often of a hundred sail apiece, striving for the windward berth. There was "team racing" at its zenith.

Once in the windward position, or "weather gauge" as it was called, it was hard for your enemy to dispossess you. With the square rigged ship it was not merely a case of putting your helm down, a slat, a flap of the sail and away on the other tack; the old ship had to be fairly coaxed round if she were in a seaway. While your modern yacht seems to want to go, the old ship seemed to be saying, "I'll be dammed if I will," and it took a man to make her go —

"Helm's alee! — Foresheet, fore top bowline, let go! — Rise tacks and sheets! — Main sail haul! — Let go and haul!" With hundreds of men to the hauling, yo-hoing and stamping, a master with a voice designed to drown two gales of wind lashed together and a boatswain with a thick stick, it would be a quarter of an hour before she was round, with everything sheeted home and bowlines taut. And, after all this struggle and commotion, six points was as near the wind as the old lady would lie.

He with the weather gauge held the master position, able to strike at once or hold off till the vital moment while he to leeward was without choice.

The fleet to windward attacked from behind a smokescreen, its movements masked, while the enemy in smoke to leeward was open to a sudden appearance of fire ships — the ancient equivalent of an attack by destroyers. While those to windward could communicate freely with their friends by signal, those to leeward were often out of touch and in consequent confusion; more often than not, they fired blind into the smoke.

Again, the lee position meant that the ships were heeled so as to expose the thin plank under the double planking at the normal water line on the engaged side; a few well placed shot here forced a ship to keep on the same tack so as to remain heeled until her people could come at the shot holes and plug them; otherwise the pierced bottom would be deeply submerged as the wind came on the other side, and down she would go like a sieve.

But the weather berth had its disadvantages.

Come a hard breeze of wind with a ship well heeled, the lower deck gun ports on her engaged side were very near the water and in a badly designed crank ship the moment came quickly when guns had to be hauled in and ports closed, thereby depriving her of her heaviest battery. Then she might be easily beaten by weight of metal; for the same hard breeze which immersed her ports was keeping those of her opponent well clear of the water on her engaged side. Ships are known to have foundered through keeping their ports open too long. On the other hand, battles have been won by men who had the tenacity to chance it with their port-sills awash and gun's crews standing in water, in the same way as today races are won in small open boats by men who have the nerve to hang on and keep going for the critical split second.

Again, a ship in the weather fleet, disabled aloft in sails and rigging and consequently unable to hold the wind with her consorts, fell helplessly to leeward among her enemies where she would be overpowered unless her friends were prepared to follow and thereby lose the advantages of position.

Most men can sail a vessel off the wind — sailors call a broad reach a soldier's wind as everyone knows — the test comes when a ship is clapped on the wind. Looking at the cumbersome old vessels of the past, modern yachtsmen, knowing nothing of the conditions imposed on the old sailing man-of-war, are inclined to suppose that the men who put up with her were incapable of understanding the refinements of sailing. But the clumsiness of gear and heaviness of design forced upon him by circumstances only made the good seaman the more eager to get the utmost out of his ship. There is a story told by a man who at one time had served as purser in Penn's squadron which is illuminating.

A frigate called the *Phoenix* had been captured by the Dutch in the Mediterranean and lay in Leghorn Roads among a squadron of her captors. By a stratagem she was cut out one dark night by Captain Owen Cox and carried clear of the Roads. By daylight it was obvious that many of the Dutch in chase were outsailing her, whereupon Cox, calling all hands on deck, asked if there were any who had before sailed in the *Phoenix*. Upon one answering that he had, "Says Cox, 'Do you know her trim?' 'Yes,' says the seaman, 'slacken her backstays, tauten this and ease that,' which they did and in six hours after ran the Dutch fleet out of sight."

We may be sure that Penn, who from youth up had used the sea, who had commanded a ship at twenty-one, was alive to all these refinements and could handle a ship with the best and toughest of the tarpaulins. He went further; having an orderly mind, he was able to handle well a squadron and in none of the big battles of the First Dutch War is there any complaint of his being out of station. Scandalmongers ashore might suggest a lack of personal courage but there was never a breath of such an accusation from those under whom he fought; indeed, when the three Generals at Sea lost one of their number by cannon shot, the survivors, Blake and Monk, specially asked that Penn should fill the vacancy; they had faith in him as a fighting seaman. In such a matter, only their opinion is worth remembering.

Penn, therefore, was a natural choice as chief-of-staff to the enthusiastic although at that time inexperienced James, Duke of York, Lord High Admiral of the fleet prepared for battle against the Dutch in the Second War of 1665. The commanders in that great assembly of squadrons and ships were a remarkable mixture of prince and pauper. Prince Rupert, who commanded the White, had been Royalist all through. Famous as a brilliant cavalry leader ashore, he had kept the royal standard flying at sea long after it had disappeared from the land; with much sea time to his credit, his command had never been anything more than a fugitive squadron living by its wits. Edward Mountagu, Earl of Sandwich, commanding the Blue squadron, had been a distinguished Parliamentary soldier who had later taken seriously to a study of naval warfare, he had previously commanded a fleet but never in action against a fleet. At the Restoration in 1660, he had changed sides with the majority and was in command of the ships which brought the King home.

Of the vice admirals, Sir John Lawson of the Red had seen most service, he was a fisherman's son and handled a pen none too well, Sir George Ayscue of the Blue was better bred, while Sir Christoper Myngs of the White boasted that his mother was a hoyman's daughter; for the rest, the officers were mostly Roundhead with a sprinkling of Cavalier. When one bright young spark of a lieutenant taunted his captain with having held a commission from Cromwell, a court martial flung him out of the Service, the order of the day being that bygones were bygones. The majority of those who in the past had conformed to the fashion of the times and sung psalms, had picked up the new tunes at the Restoration, whistling them without any apparent difficulty and there is no doubt that the personal interest of the King in his navy made for unity and a general cheerfulness.

Those who had served under Penn in Cromwell's days at the victories of the Kentish Knock, Portland, Gabbard, Texel, or at the capture of Jamaica, had sure faith that the fleet would be well handled, and he who even in Puritan days had always kept a good cellar, now drank level with the gayest of the Cavaliers when there was no work on hand. A good judge of wine was Sir William Penn.

It must have been a great day for him when the fleet got under way. At a nod from the Duke we can hear Sir William pass the word to loose the fore topsail as a sign to prepare to sail. We can see the ladies (Sir Peter Lely has left many pictures of them) being handed out of the entry port which is carved all round with loves and doves and curly things; when the pretty dears are safely in their boats, we can hear three hearty cheers from the men in the rigging, the trumpeters from the poop sounding, "Maids where are your hearts?" The boats pulled clear of the ships, the guns pay their respects. (In the *Revenge* there was tragedy when a seaman, firing too soon, killed the master's wife; the clumsy fellow was found not guilty of murder but "chance-medley;" he was whipped and put on the beach).

In the *Royal Charles* there were five hundred and fifty seamen, the master John Cox, a rousing fine seaman under whom we may be sure work went with a swing; anchor atrip, apeak and stowed, as topsails are sheeted home and trimmed, the trumpets sounding a last "Loth to depart" as the ship gathers way. Everything is coiled down and made shipshape, the watches are set as the land loses form and melts into a sea haze.

When that great fleet of over a hundred ships is brought into a single line, from the leading ship in the van to the last in the rear is a distance of some five miles; the larger ships are all aglitter with their gold wreathed ports and figureheads, the *Royal Charles* flying the royal standard at her mainmasthead as the center of a magnificent piece of sea pageantry.

In the fleet there was a goodly number of young men from the Court who had come out to see the fun (some were never to see Whitehall again). As the Dutch were not ready, the fleet was kept bucketing about in the North Sea for some weeks giving opportunity for these youngsters to learn with what constancy men needs must serve the inconstant sea, to learn something of the seaman's language (incomprehensible to the uninitiated, apt when the practice is known). The best of them learned something of that practice and all were happy enough when they had gained their sea legs; one, the Earl of Dorset, composed a ballad which has come down to us, addressed to the girls they left behind, explaining how hard it was to write:

> "Our paper, pen and ink and we
> Roll up and down our ships at sea
>
> "Then if we write not by each post
> Think not we are unkind;
> Nor yet conclude our ships are lost
> By Dutchmen or by wind:
> Our tears we'll send a speedier way,
> The tide shall bring them twice a day.
>
> "The King with wonder and surprise
> Will swear the seas grow bold;
> Because the tides will higher rise,
> Than ere they used of old:
> But let him know it is our tears
> Bring floods of grief to Whitehall stairs."

Before the final departure, there had been living on board the *Royal Charles* for a few days a grave young man of one and twenty who did not seem to fit well in the gay picture; his father sent him with despatches for the King as the fleet was about to sail; his name was William Penn.

Behind the sand dunes, the Dutchmen with less show but with grim determination made ready to wrestle for the mastery of the sea and the trade of the world; they had lost the first, they had high hopes of winning the second round. Their commander-in-chief Obdam was a brave fellow though inferior as a seaman to those of his squadron commanders, the younger Tromp and the Evertszs; the captains under them were seamen all. Of ships, there were a little over a hundred, about equal in number to the English in waiting upon them. Unfortunately for Holland, her fleet was divided into seven squadrons, each of three divisions (reflecting political division ashore) against the English nine divisions in all; twenty-one flags against nine.

On the 1st of June, when the English fleet was lying near Southwold replenishing, two of the lookouts were seen standing in from the eastward with their topgallant sheets flying. Immediately the fleet was making sail, getting into battle array as the Dutch fleet appeared on the horizon. For two days the rivals maneuvered within sight of one another but for some unexplained reason Obdam, who had the weather gauge, did not choose to fight; at dawn on June 3rd the choice was no longer his for during the night the wind, hitherto easterly, had come southwesterly.

With Rupert in the van, the English stood SE after the Dutch who, as soon as it was clear daylight, tacked and stood NW to meet them. There was a fine "chasing gale" and the two fleets lashed by one another at long range. As the Dutch rear passed, Rupert turned after them. To one critical and experienced eye on the

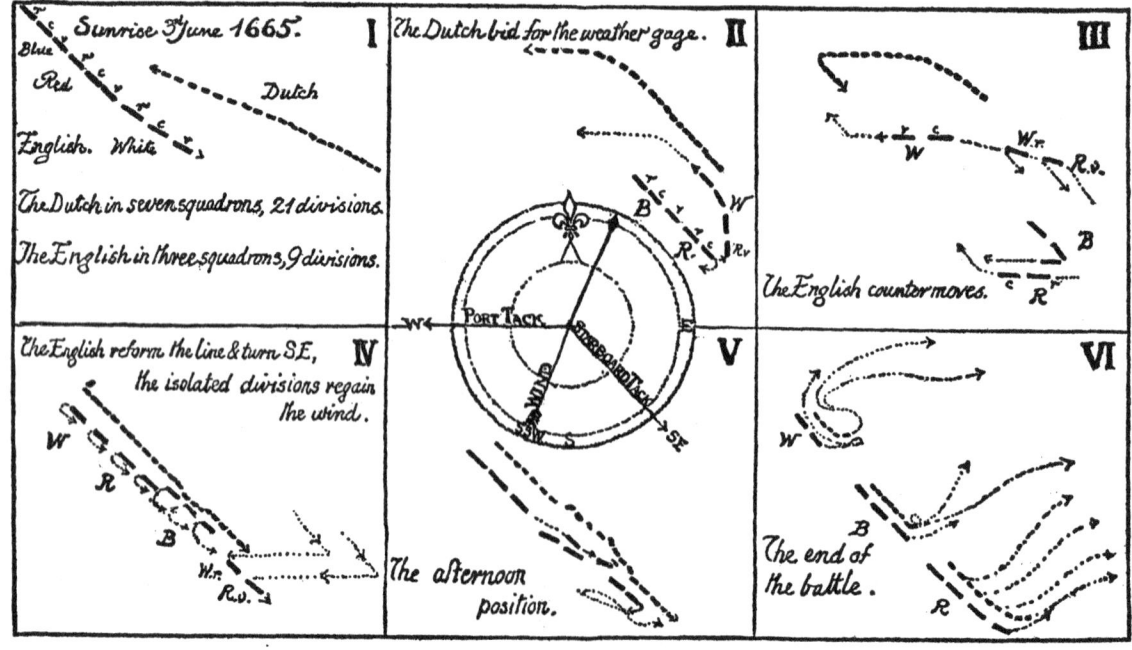

quarterdeck of the *Royal Charles* it was clear that, if the fleet were to follow in the wake of the Admiral of the White, the weather gauge would be flung away. Round came the *Royal Charles* and, keeping her luff all she could, she signalled Sandwich in the *Prince* to do the like. For the time the line was in pieces but it was well done, for when the Dutch came to the starboard tack — although Rupert with most of his squadron was able to weather them — the rear of the White together with the van of the Red were cut off to leeward. They were forced to make a long board SE before being in a position to tack again and, under Lawson's guidance in the *Royal Oak*, take station at the head of the English line, which meantime had turned together SE again. On this course, in the words of Lord Sandwich, the Dutchman "stood with us side by side and knocked it out with us for several hours".

Those Dutchmen knocked hard. Before three o'clock in the afternoon, the *Royal Oak* was beaten out of the line and tacked to the westward under the shelter of her own fleet; a message coming from Lawson to say the master was killed and he himself wounded (mortally as it proved). The veteran Jordan was sent to take command and bring her back into the line. Meanwhile Obdam in the *de Eendracht* was pressing hard the *Prince* until the *Royal Charles*, making more sail, interposed to be herself roughly handled by the Dutch flagship and the *Oranje*. The Earls of Muskerry and Falmouth and young Boyle were slain by a single chain shot, the Duke of York, who stood beside them, being covered with their blood. Dutch hopes survived until three o'clock when their flagship blew up; there were but five survivors out of five hundred. Soon afterwards, more English ships coming up, the *Oranje* was surrounded; she did not surrender until reduced to a sinking condition.

With several flag officers killed and their Commander-in-Chief destroyed, the Dutch line crumbled and Sandwich, seeing a gap, led the Blue squadron through, throwing four Dutchmen into a tangled heap; all were burned by a fire ship after refusal to surrender. Rupert in the NW was doing similar work though he had to meet an attempt to weather him before his opponents bore away for Holland. The *Marseveen*, *Tergoes* and *Swanenburg* made a last gallant effort to stem the rout but were in their turn driven together and burned. At nine o'clock at night the fight was done though the pursuit continued through the dark hours into the morning when the sandbanks of Holland brought it to an end.

Such (so far as one is able to reconcile varying accounts) was the battle of Lowestoft, costing Holland 5,000 casualties and seventeen ships against a loss of 750 and the *Charity*, which had fallen to leeward in the early stages. Criticism in Holland of the indifferent handling of her fleet was softened by Obdam's death but the lesson was understood, the defeat making for national unity which was to bear fruit in the following year. Penn, who at great pains had drafted the Duke of York's Fighting Instructions (they were to serve as a model for more than a hundred years), was doubtless disappointed in some particulars but, although there had been mixing of the squadrons, the weather gauge had been held and the line of battle maintained, thanks to a controlling mind at the centre. Victory had gone to the better handled fleet and there is no doubt to whom the credit was due for the handling.

England could hardly complain of the result, though of course the people who were not there were "definitely certain" there should have been seventy ships destroyed instead of seventeen. There was also the usual brabble as to who had done most to win the battle with the usual reckless defamation of others by the friends of some particular claimant. Surely this ever recurring post-bellum disease is the worst of the horrors of war. The shattered condition of the Red squadron protected the Duke of York from the charge of backwardness in the action but when he became unpopular politically the party politicians raked up a pretty scandal. That was two years after the event.

It appears that, after making a proper disposition of the fleet for the pursuit, the Duke and Penn had turned in for the night. Later Brouncker, one of the Duke's entourage, came on deck to suggest that, considering the fact that the Duke was next in succession to the Crown, it would be as well to avoid unnecessary personal danger and better to leave to other ships the duty of keeping touch with the enemy. Cox (the master) was asked to shorten down and, sailor like, he refused to hand a sail saying he took orders from the Duke and none else. Harman (the captain of the ship) was reluctant but, after consideration, agreed, doubtless satisfied that the frigates would do their duty in the darkness and that the service would not suffer. It was admitted that the Duke was surprised and angry when he came on deck again in the early morning and immediately ordered all sail to be made again. It was now averred that both surprise and anger were feigned, that Brouncker had spoken with his knowledge.

When Penn was asked about it he astonished them, declaring that until that moment he was unaware there had been any alteration of sail during the night; all he remembered was laboring and fighting from three in the morning till past nine at night, being much troubled with the gout and being dead dog tired. He probably yawned at the remembrance. It seems as certain as we can be certain of things happening so long ago that the charge of cowardice against the Duke was false, that for their own purposes the politicians made a mountain out of a molehill. Yet, trivial as the story is, it may be of use to us if it makes us less ready in accepting a story told against one from whom we differ in religion, politics or a taste in ties; useful if it sets us wondering whether our feelings of hatred towards an individual or a nation are not being fed by some such propaganda or other offal dished up to appear as history.

Lowestoft was Penn's last battle, his sea service drew to a close. By the fall of the year his gout grew worse and he was reluctantly asking for "the friendship of the shore for the winter." For another five years he was able to do useful work at the Admiralty, then, at the comparatively early age of forty-nine, he passed on.

Clarendon (the historian) described Penn as one who made pretense of learning and left a subject more confused by his explanation but it seems probable that Clarendon's ignorance of nautical terms had more to do with the confusion than the sailor's bad Latin. Judging by his letters, he had a weakness for Latin tags where plain English would have served. Pepys gives an entirely different impression, again and again acknowledging in the *Diary* that Penn helped him to an understanding in matters naval. There is little doubt that the reforms which later the great Secretary put forward were based largely on information supplied by him. We can the more readily accept this valuation of the professional character of Sir William because, although the two were constantly in company and outwardly friendly, Pepys was jealous of him and distrusted him as a man. He liked Lady Penn, describing her as "a well-looked fat short old Dutchwoman but one that hath been heretofore pretty handsome and is I believe very discreet and hath more wit than her husband." He was obviously fond of Peg Penn and for young William, who in the *Diary* time was already exhibiting unorthodox religious and political views, he had kindly feelings, probably saving him from a second thrashing from his heavy handed parent. But Father Penn is written down "a false and mean fellow," and unfortunately there is to be found elsewhere support for so bitter a censure.

It may be that, when as Rear Admiral serving the Parliament he was suspected of correspondence with the Royalists, there was no more ground for suspicion than a friendliness with those who had suddenly changed sides; it may be that, when five years later Cromwell wrote what reads as a friendly warning that he was again suspect, there were no grounds for mistrust; but there is no doubt at all that in the following year Penn was offering to take the fleet entrusted to him by the Protector into any port Charles (then in exile) might name. Cromwell's suspicion that there was something in the wind seems to have been confirmed in 1655, for in that year he deprived Penn of his commission as one of the Generals at Sea, though he permitted him to retain the confiscated Royalists' estates in Ireland which had been his reward for services rendered to the Commonwealth. Unfortunately for his good name, William Penn, Senior, retained them.

A hundred years later, Granville Penn seemed to think that by heaping abuse upon Cromwell he was clearing his great-grandfather's reputation. Stripped down, the drift of his defense seems to lead to this: in dealing with a knave an upright man is justified in acting dishonorably. Unfortunately the assumption that another is dishonest is, by the man who has already dubbed himself a man of honor, assumption arising out of dubiety. In any case, it is not good for a man to make personal profit out of vice.

Monk, Sandwich, Lawson and many other seamen had changed sides but none of them had taken rewards from Cromwell and corresponded with the Royalists at the same time. Although they all admired Penn's outstanding efficiency and single-mindedness in the Service of the sea, they wished it had not been crossed in his private conduct with a streak of acquisitiveness — a quality ranking seemingly as a virtue in some walks of life but foreign to the character of the naval officer. They knew him to be incapable of the utter baseness of treachery against brothers-in-arms on the day of battle but they wished he had minded the words of one of their number —"'Tis not for us to mind state affairs but to keep foreigners from fooling us."

We may wonder how much of that unjust suspicion which later for a while shadowed the Quaker could be traced to a knowledge of his father's double-dealing; it was, of course, in the remembrance of many. Certain it is that the memory of his Dutch mother, "pretty handsome and very discreet," was as a leading mark to the founder of Pennsylvania in his voyage through life while his father's career seemed to him more as a wreck upon a shoal to warn him of danger. Yet it is doubtful whether he would have fetched so far had there not been something of the character of the old man in him. For young William Penn came to pursue peace with as much pugnacity as his father had waged war, to write his controversial religious and political pamphlets with as much force as the admiral had fired his broadsides in battle and, as the sailor had gone to sea thinking to break away from the bondage of the shore, so the Quaker, revolting from the political turmoil and religious rancor of home, sailed westward looking for wider spaces, where the spirit might hope to find greater freedom, to the land he wished to call Sylvannia. It was King Charles II who insisted on the prefix, "in memory" he said "of your father, Admiral Sir William Penn."

XI

THE ENDEAVOUR

For illustration, see frontispiece

THE ENDEAVOUR

*How Captain Cook Opened Up the Pacific and Discovered
the Northwestern Coast of America*

OLD seafaring books tell us that from time immemorial the coal trade on
the east coast of England has been an excellent nursery for seamen.
Those whose business has been in the North Sea will know why, while
the others will gain an inkling by an examination of the chart of the waters 'twixt
Tyne and Thames.

From Newcastle to Flamborough Head is a jagged steep shore where sound-
ings are of little help, and on a murky night a sharp lookout is the seaman's main
guard, for otherwise he may easily find himself butt against unscalable cliffs between two casts of the lead. So you go for eighty miles, then a sudden change.
South of Flamborough the coast lies low, no marks can be seen, and sandbanks
stretch out afar. Here, in the days before lightvessels and high-powered lights
ashore, the seaman had need to use his lead as the blind man uses his stick — tap,
tap, all the way to London town. Visibility being generally poor in the North Sea,
the young seaman has always been well schooled in his "three L's" — lookout,
lead, and log. Small wonder that in the old days they were all good who came out
of it; the others were drowned.

James Cook, the seamen's seaman, was a survivor of this nursery. He was no
come-by-chance hero. True, he came of poor parentage as the world reckons,
but they were none so poor that they did not endow him with a stout heart, a good
digestion, and a mind able for the storage of experience; that is inheritance
enough. It is likely that this child of a moorland farm became weatherwise soon
after he started crow-scaring which was not long after he had learned to walk.
We may suppose that as assistant in the little general store at Staithes, where he
weighed sugar by the pound and cut off tape by the yard for the fishwives, he laid
the foundation of that quality of accuracy with which long after he measured
up this old world of ours. Doubtless, the old ladies never had inch nor ounce
more than what they had paid for; he was always exact, was Captain James
Cook.

We know that come green shutter time at the shop he was away down among
the fishermen, lending a hand to haul the cobles in and out at the Staith, learning
that close intimacy with the way of a ship which can be acquired only by early
practice in small craft. We may reckon that the first time young James was sent
ashore at Wapping for stores for the collier *Freelove*, wherein he came to be bound,
he brought the boat back alongside without waking the skipper in his bunk.

Handiness in a boat was more thought of in those days than many school certificates.

Old King Coal has never allowed the ships in his service much time in harbor, so that for nigh ten years we can picture young Cook in foul wind and fair, wet and shine, gathering experience as boy, man, and mate. As mate, doubtless he made his own corrections on the crude charts, and annotated the simple sailing directions of the day. Then, when he was in a fair way to become a master in the coal trade, suddenly, as it seemed, he stepped on board H.M.S. *Eagle* to volunteer as an able seaman. That was in 1755.

The earlier biographers insist that he joined in a hurry to avoid being forced by the press gang, as they also insist that he had earlier run away to sea after helping himself to a shilling out of the till. None of this seems to fit into the pattern of the man's life and it is not surprising, therefore, that Kitson — who went to some trouble — found that none of these things happened. It is known that Sanderson, the grocer of Staithes, went with his assistant into Whitby to arrange his apprenticeship to the sea, and remained always on friendly terms. As to his entry into the Navy, there is evidence that it had been long in contemplation and that his friends the shipowners had been told of the intention some time before.

He was seven and twenty, standing well over six feet, spare, but hard as nails — his mother was of Cleveland where the iron comes from. A firm mouth and steady eye, he was of the sort that cannot be overlooked, and within six weeks of joining the *Eagle* he was made master's mate. As such he served for two years, gaining the regard of the master and Captain Palliser. Sir Hugh Palliser was to survive to raise a noble monument to this man who had entered the ship as an A.B. In 1757 came his appointment to the *Pembroke* as master. In her he was engaged at Louisburg and, in 1759, when she went up the St. Lawrence, Cook was selected to carry out under fire the survey and buoyage of the channel whereby Wolfe went his way to victory and death at Quebec.

This work was done under the eye of the Admiral and led to appointment as master of the flagship where he found time to study higher mathematics and the principles underlying practical surveying, thereby fitting himself for duties beyond those of an ordinary sailing master. Opportunity came quickly. When the war ceased, the Governor of Newfoundland asked for and obtained his services as "King's Surveyor" and the next four years were devoted to a complete survey of the island and its approaches. Considering the great difficulties under which the task was carried out, the charts are remarkable in their accuracy. In 1767, the man who but twelve years before had come in through the hawsepipes, who had already proved himself a man of iron resolution, had the pleasure of hearing that the results of some of his astronomical observations had been laid before the polite and learned Royal Society. A rare compound of a man was James Cook.

About the time he was finishing the North American work, the Royal Society was asking the Admiralty to fit out a vessel with the intention of observing the transit of Venus at Tahiti. The Admiralty had sent two expeditions recently to the Pacific whose main purpose had been the discovery of a great southern continent always believed to exist for the purpose of holding this world of ours right end up. There being so much land in the Northern Hemisphere, it was argued that there must be corresponding land in the south — an early example, perhaps, of belief in the efficacy of outside ballast. Commanded by gallant naval captains, the ships had returned with sadly reduced crews, the survivors weakened with scurvy, no news of the continent, and generally with meager scientific results. Lord Hawke at the Admiralty was pressed, in any new expedition, to give the command to a scien-

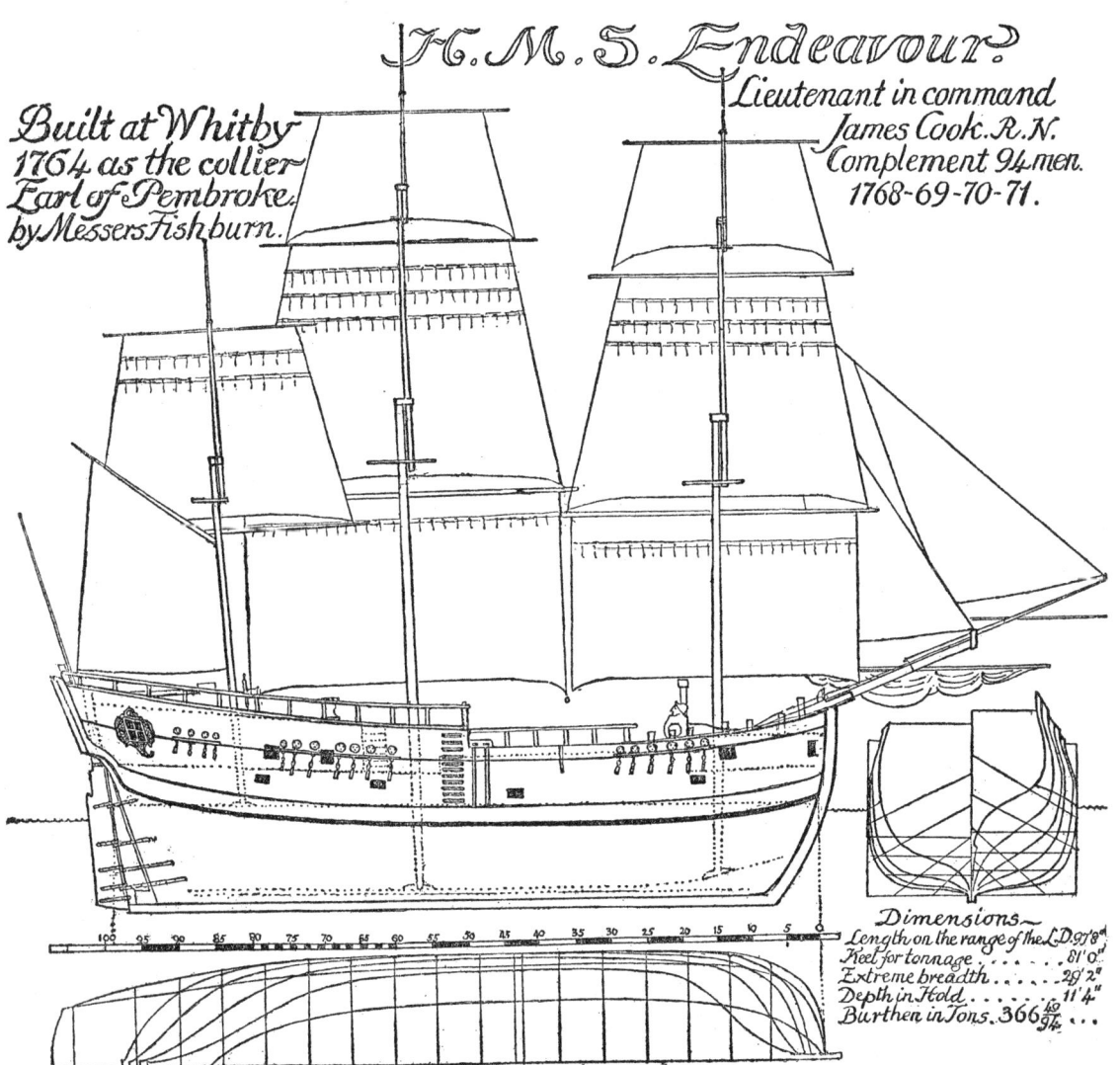

H.M.S. Endeavour

Built at Whitby 1764 as the collier Earl of Pembroke by Messers Fishburn.

Lieutenant in command
James Cook. R.N.
Complement 94 men.
1768-69-70-71.

Dimensions ~
Length on the range of the L.D. 97'8"
Keel for tonnage . . . . 81'0"
Extreme breadth . . . . . . 29'2"
Depth in Hold . . . . 11'4"
Burthen in Tons. 366 40/94 . . .

tist, who was nominated. The First Lord agreed that a scientist was needed but insisted that he must be a seaman too. Hawke had his eye on one man — James Cook. In those days the masters in the Navy held their posts by warrant; it was necessary, therefore, to give Cook a comission as lieutenant before he could take command. There was never a happier choice made.

With good sense, the choice of vessels was left to the man who was to do the work and the one-time collier's boy chose a collier. When she was brought to dry-dock at Deptford, we may imagine she came as something of a shock to the government shipwrights. They were used to ships with cod's heads and mackerel's tails; Cook's fancy had a bow like a hammer-headed shark and a tail that did not begin much before it was time to leave off. Plainly, so far as mold went, she was in direct descent from the dugout. The modern designer looking at her lines finds it hard to believe that such a vessel could get 'round. She did get 'round, bringing with her documentary evidence of handiness, for Cook's charts show plainly that she was often in tight corners, to get out of which a ship had need to be handy. Obviously, she was slow; in a three-year voyage her best day's run was but 160 miles. She rolled; we know that her larger sister in the second voyage rolled 38° each way when running in a breeze. She was strong; the only time she was badly aground it was her strength which saved her. As for her looks, it will be seen from the plan that she had need to comfort herself with the old saw, "Handsome is as handsome does."

Apart from Cook's natural faith in the type in which he had spent his youth, the qualities which made the collier preferable to the alternative twenty-gun ship were a larger hold and a greater loftiness between decks where the men were to be berthed. Within the 97 feet which was her length between perpendiculars, he intended to stow eighteen months' provisions and to keep in health 94 people. Time out of mind that scourge of seamen, scurvy had brought to nought much endeavor at sea; in his *Endeavour* — so they had named his ship — he was determined that disease should be fought with all available forces. Fresh air, light and cleanliness below, fresh food whenever obtainable, otherwise the best known substitutes — these were the weapons which the better medical brains of the day recommended to him for the fight, so that extra stowage for a barrel of lemon juice or a cask of sauerkraut, and an extra cubic foot of air space, seemed to him more than worth while. True, he did not originate these ideas, but he was the first man to put them into practice. "Friday, September 16th, 1768, punished Henry Stevens, seaman, and Thomas Dunster, marine, with 12 lashes each for refusing to take their allowance of fresh beef. Wind easterly." So runs an early entry in Cook's journal. While tender-hearted modern dietitians may consider their great forerunner a heavy-handed practitioner, I suspect that they will secretly envy the power to give such peremptory treatment.

The details of the *Endeavour's* voyage and the two succeeding voyages in the *Resolution* have been told over and over again; here it would be useless to attempt anything more than a brief summary. Briefly, then, the *Endeavour* was to make first for Tahiti, by way of Cape Horn, for the astronomical work. This done, she was to search for the continent with that gaudy name — Terra Australis Incognita. You can see how of necessity a country with such a lengthy appellation would have need to appear large on the maps. On the old globes it sprawled right 'round and poked up as near the equator as 30° S, while New Zealand, which old Tasman had sighted in 1642 and none had seen since, was reckoned a spur of it. If he drew a blank in the hunt south from Tahiti, Cook was to make for New Zealand. As a matter of fact, he was convinced by deduction when he had penetrated 600 leagues into the Pacific that there was no land of consequence to the southward; nevertheless, he struck south before standing to the westward in pursuance of orders and out of politeness, we may suppose, for other people's theories.

New Zealand was sighted about halfway up the east coast of North Island. After making a short hitch south to a headland he called Cape Turnagain, he stood to the northward, charting and landing where he could. Battling 'round Cape Maria van Diemen, in weather which he admitted was as bad as any he had ever experienced, he yet fixed the Cape's position accurately before turning south along the west coast, where, in a succession of westerly gales, the little collier clawed along the dead lee shore. The chart is evidence of the Captain's daring, his journal makes clear how that daring was finely balanced with prudence. He and his men had been tried to the limit and it must have been a great relief when what appeared to be a great bay opened out to receive them.

Landing, not long after the ship was made snug in a cove, and climbing a hill, Cook discovered they had fallen into the strait which now bears his name. Later, passing through, he stood north as far as Cape Turnagain, at sight of which he called all his officers on deck and pointed it out to them. Then, being assured that they recognized it and were satisfied that there had been complete circumnavigation, he turned away to sail around South Island without landing until he came again into the strait. Bad weather prevented him often from closing the land; he mistook Bank's Peninsula for an island and failed to separate Stewart Island, but he left in both chart and journal indication of all uncertainties. In all his work he modestly claimed no more than that it was the best he could do under the circumstances, warning seamen of possible errors. Yet, in spite of his having no chronometer on this first voyage, his longitudes are rarely more than a few miles out, and in the case of New Zealand the chart is a wonderful approximation.

After New Zealand, the orders gave a free hand and Cook decided to pick up another of Tasman's loose ends. That great Dutch pioneer had sighted Tasmania on his passage east. Cook stood away west, therefore, sighting the north end of it and turning northerly to pick up the Australian coast at a point he named Cape Howe. Here began his second great survey; the 2000-mile coast which no white man had ever seen before was charted within four months.

When one looks at the chart of the Queensland coast one is amazed that the little ship came through the tangle of reefs, passing where ships have never cared to navigate since. Cook prudently moved in daylight only, but one bright moon-light night, being tempted to carry on, he found himself hard and fast on a reef near the point feelingly named Cape Tribulation. The ship was badly holed; guns, ballast and stores were flung overboard, lightening her fifty tons, topmasts struck, and anchors laid out. Everything was done which a prime seaman with a fine ship's company working under him could do. For twenty-four hours all were striving; then, as the tide rose, the ship righted. The pumps were going, the leak was gaining on them. There was the chance of a change in the weather with the certainty of the ship breaking up if she remained; there was no certainty that she would float if she came off. The *Endeavour* was just a lone ship lying aground twenty miles from an unknown coast. "However, I resolved to risk all and heave her off —" so Cook writes in his simple account of the affair. With alternate hopes and fears, they covered the distance to the shore to find a haven where they beached her, and in six weeks she was repaired in a rough and ready manner. One more close call, this time outside the Barrier Reef, and then away she went through Torres Strait for Batavia.

Hitherto, Monkhouse and Perry, the surgeons, with their captain always behind them, had kept the men in health; but now while the ship was hove down and repairing, the men, who were all living ashore, contracted dysentery. Many were buried in Batavia, Monkhouse among them; those who returned to carry the ship home were the ghosts of themselves and many passed away on the passage to the Cape. It was a sad disappointment to Cook, making him querulous and a little ungenerous to the memory of some who had served him well. Doubtless many of those who died had not been too careful of health at the first contact with civilization after so long an absence, but one could wish the fact had been left unnoted in the journal. Temperate himself, he could never understand the slightest divergence in others, could never forgive anything which checked "the service upon which they were engaged."

The *Endeavour's* circumnavigation brought a full harvest. If the vision of Terra Australis Incognita had faded out for most sensible people, New Holland and New Zealand had been raised clear of the mist and became realities. Many new islands had been discovered in the Pacific and all had been well charted. Cook summarized in his journal the work yet to be done and a paraphrase of this summary became his orders for another voyage. He was to make a complete circumnavigation in high southern latitudes.

On this second voyage eastabout, he sailed in the *Resolution,* with the *Adventure,* a smaller collier, for company; his peril on the Australian coast had taught him the value of a consort. Nevertheless, when the two ships lost company and the *Adventure* went home, Cook was not diverted from his resolution to probe and probe into the Antarctic as far south as ever the icefields would allow the ship to go. Alone in the fog and snow — snow so thick that often they shook the *Resolution* up into the wind to get the snow out of her topsails. So they struggled on until, as he wrote, "even my spirit was broken." Between times the crew recuperated and made merry at Tahiti, while the tireless and austere navigator checked over his work and thought of home.

Three years and eighteen days after her departure the *Resolution* returned with the loss of a single man due to sickness out of a crew of 118. That alone was an unheard of accomplishment and the beginning of a new era in naval hygiene. The geographical results were mainly negative. Terra Australis Incognita, that land capable of supporting fifty million people, as it had been supposed, had been finally wiped off the map. It had been proved that whatever land there might be was close around the Pole and useless for colonization. The Southern Hemisphere ceased to be a land and sea of make believe, and outside the Antarctic Circle it remains today, in the main, as Cook charted it.

In 1775, when he returned, Cook was 47 and he would have been wise perhaps had he devoted the rest of his life to science ashore. But a call came in the following year and he went to sea again in the *Resolution,* this time with the *Discovery* as consort. His orders were to attempt the discovery, from the Pacific side, of navigable ways north, about Asia and America — both age-old problems. The two ships proceeded by way of the Cape of Good Hope to the old haunts, the Southern Pacific Islands. Then, at the latter end of 1777, they stood away north to discover, on Christmas Eve, the island which bears that happy name. Then, steering north, on the 18th of January, 1778, the lookouts descried snow-capped mountainous land as a cloud dead ahead. That was the white man's first view, after an interval of two hundred years, of what we now know as the Hawaiian Islands. He realized the outstanding importance to Pacific navigation of the group but stayed only a short time, knowing that he must strike at the Arctic at the right season. The American coast was made at Vancouver Island. Though he failed to separate the isle from the main, it may be claimed that he opened the western gate of Canada; as we have seen, he had already lent a hand in the opening of the eastern gate. Bad weather persisting, he was driven much off the land to come in again and again, searching for an opening, laying down on the chart all he saw. On through Bering Strait to the ice, far enough north to be convinced and to record that there was no useful way north about America. Then came the return to Hawaii for the winter season and here it was that the great navigator came to Journey's End.

Clerke, who succeeded to the command, was then a dying man but, with a magnificent spirit, he returned to the north. He carried on long after the people knew there could be no navigable channel, probably long after he, too, realized there was no way, but, lest his weakness might seem to influence a decision to turn, this fine fellow persisted. At last, to the great relief of all, he ordered the ships about, and died a few weeks afterwards off the Kamchatka coast. Years before, he had joined the old *Endeavour* as an able seaman, to return home in her as an acting lieutenant; he had served again in the second voyage. A right worthy follower was Captain Charles Clerke.

Such is a brief record of the achievement of Captain James Cook, leaving out all concerning the manners and customs of the natives, the wonders of natural history, and the astronomical data gathered and brought to book by the devoted workers under his command. Previous navigators had gone round the world, more as children seeking adventure — often, it must be said, as greedy children robbing orchards on the way. Cook had no time for orchard robbing, and adventure was just an incidental nuisance; in his journal he testily remarks that people often write "as if the whole merit of the voyage consisted in the dangers and hardships they underwent." It was a grown man who sailed in the *Endeavour*, out for knowledge, out for the giving of fair measure, out to make the paths straight for all seamen, all ships.

That the man himself had failings, that contacts with some temperaments sometimes brought his temper to hurricane force, and that at its full his natural upstanding sense of justice momentarily bent before it, we can accept, without believing for one moment that he was generally unjust, savage and unbearable. The presence in the last voyage of Charles Clerke and of that other old *Endeavour* Captain, John Gore, to whom was to fall the honor of bringing the ships home is sufficient answer to such a charge. He would have been too good to be true had he been admired by all the company with whom he sailed, but it is remarkable that he held the respect of two such diversities as Sir Joseph Banks and Master William Bligh.

Old Admiral Isaac Smith told one story to the end of his days. When, at the first landing, the keel of the *Endeavour's* boat grated on the beach of New South Wales and all stood waiting for the famous navigator to step ceremoniously ashore, he turned to young Smith, then a midshipman, with a cheery "Jump out, Isaac." Perhaps to those who set great store on the vanities of Church and State, Cook's behavior will appear undignified and altogether too homely for such a great occasion; others will see in it a gentleness and a kindliness unexpected from one usually so stern and unbending.

Certain it is that Cook does not figure here as one of the heroes of antiquity, nor as a man sent out primarily to conquer new lands, but none ever supposed that such was the intent until a few years ago when we were asked to accept that in the first voyage science was but a cloak to hide an expedition of British acquisitiveness. Significance was attached to the fact that the *Endeavour's* secret orders remained unpublished until recent times and that among them was an order to take possession of any new lands discovered. Further, it was suggested that the news of a Spanish military occupation of Juan Fernandez, brought home by Carteret in the *Swallow*, was the immediate inspiration of this particular paragraph and we were twitted with being altogether too simple-minded if we believed that the British Admiralty had any real interest in scientific research.

As there is an identical paragraph in the *Resolution's* orders for the third voyage, at which time the King of France, who warred with England, gave order to his Navy to let Cook go his way in peace, and Franklin asked Congress that a like courtesy might be extended by America, it would follow that these two countries were being fooled; it would follow that an act of chivalry so rare in history was being flung away on a nation unworthy. Were it not that the occasion when this new estimate was brought forward was the bicentenary celebration held by the Royal Geographical Society, it might well be passed over in silence, but since time and circumstance may give it some credit among those who have little faith in humanity, it would be as well, perhaps, to hold formal inquest before interment.

As measure of the recklessness of this new estimate, it may be stated at once that when the *Endeavour* sailed in August, 1768, the *Swallow* had not been heard of for years. She was believed lost and eventually limped into Plymouth months afterwards. Anything, therefore, the gallant Carteret knew could have had no influence on Cook's orders. As to there being any significance in the non-publication of the *Endeavour's* orders, we know that those of the *Resolution*, with a similar paragraph, were broadcast before peace was declared. We may infer by their actions that Byron, Wallis and Carteret each sailed under a like instruction and that the same applies to the explorers of the day of whatever nationality. In fact, it has been common to all orders given before or since.

As to the incredulity with which we are asked to treat the genuineness of the British Admiralty's interest in science, it is to be noted that of those who signed Cook's orders, two were seamen who might be expected to take keen interest in the construction of accurate charts and in any matter which advanced nautical astronomy; even the third, Lord Spencer, who understood better the points of a horse than the lines of a ship, might have guessed that there was some use in these things. But if this were not so, and to their minds the prime objects of the voyage were military and real estate, what possessed them, one wonders, to take a man of non-military rank, a known hydrographer, and place him in command, cluttering up his ship with botanists, naturalists, astronomers and, of all people, artists! What were they all doing in a war galley?

And when Cook came home after these long years and admitted he had spent most of the time laboriously sounding and charting, even his claim that he had planted flags in New Zealand and New South Wales would not have saved him from the censure of his sword-clanking acquisitive masters. But he was not court-martialed. Instead, they promoted him and sent him out to do the same thing over again. The politicians of the Eighteenth Century may have had a hard casing of materialism, but underneath was something more impressionable. They realized surely, that by helping on the work of their servant they were winning larger and more lasting honor for their country than ever could be won by territorial aggrandizement.

Beyond question, in the mind and heart of James Cook scientific work ever stood first; and although he was happy in the thought that his own people would one day inhabit those spacious countries lying beneath the Southern Cross, as he sailed along their shores his vision was of a peaceful land with corn growing and sheep grazing tended by a contented people. There was never in him the spirit of an aggressive imperialism.

He had been south looking for Terra Australis Incognita, to find instead a waste of waters possessed by boisterous seas which swung unchecked right around the world. There he may have minded a line of Shakespeare's — "What care these roarers for the name of King." He had been star gazing, too, in Tahiti, gaining thereby a glimmering of the extent of the universe, a sense of the larger proportions in time and space — it was not likely that in his mind empire would be confused with eternity. Such men can never be held within narrow political boundaries; they are out to serve mankind. There is hope for a world wherein such men are honored.

XII

THE BON HOMME RICHARD

THE BON HOMME RICHARD, 1778

THE BON HOMME RICHARD

*How Commander Jones' Squadron Alarmed the Enemy's
Coast from Leith to Flamborough Head*

IT IS THE FATE of all men destined to become popular naval heroes to be
made fools of in the process of being made popular, and John Paul Jones is no
exception to the rule of which Nelson is the classical example. For more than
a hundred years the famous admiral was represented as having behaved like a fool
at the onset of his crowning victory. Eventually the British Admiralty decided to
appoint a Committee to discover what, in fact, his tactics were at Trafalgar in
1805 and, as a result, a Blue Book was published in 1913 vindicating his character
as a wise commander. It does not seem beyond the bounds of possibility that some
day the Navy Department of the United States may be moved to take a similar
step in the case of John Paul Jones.

In Nelson's case he used to be represented as having approached the Franco-
Spanish fleet in such a manner as to give it an opportunity of annihilating his leading ships without their having a chance to hit back. In Jones' case he is represented to have attacked a superior force of disciplined well-armed ships, himself in
a hopelessly lumbering, ill-conditioned vessel, with consorts commanded by men
who were known to him as either mutinous, cowardly, lunatic or neurotic — so
these gentlemen are described in various accounts.

In each case these alleged displays of foolishness are put forward for no other
discoverable reason than to exhibit valor as the one essential martial virtue. They
gain credence because in some mysterious way acts of foolhardiness appeal more
strongly than anything else to national vanity. The logical deduction is, of course,
that, forethought being unnecessary, brains in a sea commander are redundant.
Surely the blessed modern word "bunk" was invented specially to describe doctrine such as this. Certainly it was not the doctrine of Captain John Paul Jones,
who is a shining example of one who thought hard like a chess player before he
moved into a position where he knew his valor would have a fair chance of winning.

On his first appearance as an American naval officer in British waters he confined his operations to that portion of them which, as man and boy in the British
merchant service, he had learned inside out. The cruise through the Irish Sea in
the *Ranger* was in effect a piece of range-finding to test whether the slackness and
overconfidence on the coasts had been replaced by watchfulness. At Whitehaven,
where he went in and spiked the guns and was away again before cockcrow, he had
his answer — there was no opposition for everybody was asleep. With the guardship

Drake there was a short sharp tussle, but the slackness and unreadiness not un-
common in small detached men-of-war would have been well known to Paul Jones;
had the result been other than it was, he would have been much surprised.

Being an intelligent man, he knew that while the affair at Whitehaven might
pass as a military exploit of magnitude among the thoughtless, among the more
reflective it would not count for much, for they would quickly hold up a mirror
and see the whole picture in reverse — a native-born American who from boyhood
had sailed out of, say, Baltimore in Maryland, suddenly becoming enamored of
the beauties of the British Constitution and, after an interval of a few years, sailing under the British flag into his old home port on a dark night, to do what damage he might before daylight. He knew, too, that a string of merchant prizes was
the usual harvest of the ordinary privateersman and would give him no distinction. But he knew that to capture in fair stand up fight a man-of-war was an entirely different matter and likely to make a stir. So with fine dramatic sense he
gave up further profitable cruising for prize to make a spectacular entry into the
port of Brest with His Britannic Majesty's sloop of war *Drake* tucked under his
stern.

I think of late years Paul Jones' vanity has been a little too much insisted
upon at the expense of his consuming ambition. No doubt he enjoyed the adulation received to the full, but the gaining of it was but a means to an end, an end he
had in view when he set out across the Atlantic in the little *Ranger*, and before
that.

I suspect that John Paul, the small Scots gardener's boy of Arbigland, had a
bright vision of Admiral John Paul Jones wearing his flag as Commander-in-Chief
of a superb fleet, even before he was tall enough to look over the tops of the
chrysanthemums as they bloomed in his native Kirkcudbrightshire.

Previous to his successful cruise in the *Ranger* he had made a short trial in
America but had soon realized that his progress there was likely to be slow, for the
hard set Puritan stock had ever breathed independence; to them it was no new
demand, and now all they asked was to be left alone. They had looked with suspicion on this young Scottish convert to the cause who breathed revenge, and
they wished him gone.

In France, where his fascinating personality seems to have had a devastating
effect on the fair ladies of the Court of Louis XVI and Marie Antoinette, he could
hope with confidence that progress would be more rapid, for here enmity was
hereditary against England; enmity losing nothing in the rebound. War had been
a habit for hundreds of years. "War" was the slogan and war was John Paul
Jones' only way to glory.

Thus it came about that on the 14th of August, 1779, there sailed out beyond
the castles flaunting the golden lilies of old France a squadron of ships displaying

the star spangled banner of the new nation with the intent of bringing war to the very gates of proud, perfidious, tyrannical Albion.

As flagship was the twelve-year-old French Indiaman *Duc de Duras*, renamed *Bon Homme Richard*, rearmed and rerigged under the eye of Jones himself. She was not perfect, though doubtless before he finished his work he saw that she was pretty good. The new American-built frigate *Alliance*, Captain Pierre Landais; the French-built frigate *Pallas*, Captain Cottineau; the brig *Vengeance*, Captain Ricot; and the cutter *Cerf* made up the squadron. There were besides two fine French privateers. As they soon parted company, we need not burden memory with their names.

The squadron sailed with a fine bunch of blessings from the fair. Unfortunately, Paul Jones had permitted himself to ship a curse in the form of a "Concordat" which he seems to have understood gave commanders under him leave to come and go at their fancy. Why he signed such an agreement and respected it is a mystery unsolvable by those who like to compare the seaman with Napoleon. The Corsican might have signed such a document but, as soon as the land had dipped out of sight, he would have drowned any mother's son who had dared to quote it.

The British Government, whose secret agents walked about France juggling golden guineas in their pockets, was advised of the squadron's departure. Other information gathered from "people who knew" was that Liverpool would be the chief point of attack. We may be sure that port was well guarded and Whitehaven, too, kept awake of nights. There was nervousness at the seat of the Earl of Selkirk nearby, where, in the *Ranger's* cruise, the crew had helped themselves to a silver tea-service, afterwards to be restored by her romantic captain with apologies to her ladyship the Countess.

Needless to say the squadron left all the lookouts in the Irish Sea looking and, unlooked for, sailed up the West coast of Ireland, passing north about Scotland to find the eastern coast line unprotected. Landais in the *Alliance*, using the "Concordat" to the full, appeared and disappeared as he chose; he was missing, as was the *Cerf*, when one of the set pieces of the expedition was due to be performed. This was no other than the capture of Leith, port of the capital of Scotland, and from Edinburgh it was proposed to levy £200,000.

But the three ships were never to fetch the length of Leith Roads. After two days spent turning up the Firth of Forth, during which time the whole countryside became alarmed, the wind increased to gale force. Reluctantly the attempt was given over, it is said on the advice of the two other captains, Cottineau and Ricot, though one may suspect, the element of surprise gone, the Commodore with all his optimism realized that the issue had become doubtful. He would have remembered how at Whitehaven, with an American ship's company, there had been failure to carry out his orders and now on board the *Richard* was an extraordinary collection from all the nations. Under the eye of their indomitable captain, they behaved well but, once out of sight and beyond his hypnotic power — as many would be in a combined land and sea operation — their value as a fighting force was problematical. One reads much in the history books of the panic amongst Edinburgh people and it seems to be generally assumed that there would have been a poor resistance — an assumption quite incredible to those who know anything of the record of Scotland.

A failure to persuade Cottineau to back an attempt on the Tyne was an added disappointment and, although he had the satisfaction of a string of prizes, there had been no outstanding action to further his ambition. It was a somewhat disappointed Paul Jones who passed Scarborough on his way south towards Flamborough Head, the final rendezvous of the cruise before returning to France.

But on the 22nd of September fortune smiled on him again. From the Humber pilots who hung about the headland he heard of the approach of the "Baltic Trade," and that it was likely to be a rich fleet. Doubtless he extracted from his prisoner pilots the probable strength of the escorting vessels; he may even have learned their names. On the morning of the 23rd the *Alliance* reappeared, so that his squadron now numbered four, and the Commodore awaited with equanimity the advent of the convoy.

The good people of Scarborough had seen him pass. It does not appear that they were aware of his identity though they recognized him as an enemy and were duly thankful at his passing. When, early on the following morning, the British convoy of forty ships swept by, the Bailiff sent a warning to the senior officer, Captain Richard Pearson in the *Serapis*, 44 guns, who had stood close in, probably on the off chance of getting a fisherman to convey letters ashore to acquaint sweethearts and wives of a safe return to home waters. Many sweethearts and wives were going to be disappointed.

Immediately on hearing intelligence of an enemy, Pearson made the signal to the convoy to come under his lee. But Flamborough is 35 miles north of Humber, which was home for many of the fleet, and the leaders kept stretching out and looking ahead, taking no notice of the signal. Pearson sent the *Countess of Scarborough*, 22 guns, Captain Thomas Piercy, to hail as many as he could and compel instant obedience, he himself cracking on all sail to get up with the leaders; soon after noon he observed these letting fly topgallant sheets (indicating an enemy in sight) and coming down helter-skelter to gain his protection.

It was past four o'clock in the afternoon before the cause of all the flapping and scuttering was visible from the *Serapis'* deck. It then appeared to Pearson that he had to deal with a two-decker, two frigates and a brig, an addition of one frigate to the account he had received from Scarborough in the early morning.

This made a difference as to his expectations of the issue but it made no difference in his action. There he was bound by an iron Regulation. Signalling to the convoy to tack and to his small consort to rejoin, together these two stood away south towards the approaching squadron with a gentle but steady southwesterly breeze.

Whatever his previous knowledge may have been, the tacking of the forty ships in the convoy now revealed to Paul Jones the forces opposed to him. It must have reminded him of his actor days; the crowd, making "exit left," leaving the stage to the two principal characters. One of them made a fine showing with the setting sun gilding her starboard side, for the *Serapis* was an almost new 44-gun ship. He would recognize her class at once, for it was distinctive. Neither line of battle ship nor frigate, this ancient type had been revived because it was particularly suited for convoy work demanding a ship handy yet heavy enough in gun power to chase away and overawe the frigates and light privateersmen who commonly hung around ready to pounce on stragglers. He knew that in the ordinary way such a ship with no responsibilities could hold a ship like his bulkier *Richard* at long range and silence her. He knew that, with night coming on and a superiority in number of ships against him, Pearson dare not play at long bowls but must come to close range at once and endeavor to get a prompt settlement of the account.

Paul Jones was no fool. He foresaw the critical period in the coming conflict, and an anxious period for him, during which he was likely to receive terrible punishment from an opponent with a heavier punch and a longer reach; but he also knew that surviving it and closing, superiority would swing right over to his side, with a ship full of men, boarding pikes, grenades and muskets. Sure of himself, with his unbounded self-confidence and optimism he felt himself able to hold up his people through the precarious minutes.

Failure could not be contemplated, for it was not for effect he had said he would be hanged if he were caught; it certainly would not be for love of his grey eyes that he would be spared. There would be the fear of reprisals on British prisoners in America and his commission to protect him certainly, but there was an old charge of causing the death of one of his crew when in command of a British ship, and upon that a fair trial could hardly be hoped for in war time. It was a very brave man who commanded the ship *Bon Homme Richard* on that beautiful September evening in 1779.

The sun was sinking behind Flamborough. At six, the two British ships came to the port tack with their heads towards the land, thus bringing the antagonists on converging courses and making it possible to gauge the approximate time of contact; about seven, Jones reckoned. Twilight lasts two hours in the latitude of Flamborough and that night the moon was full. There was going to be a little too much light for his purpose, but it would be a confused light and he could congratulate himself on having timed the meeting very well.

Seven o'clock and the *Serapis* was near enough to open fire had she chosen. There was neither sound nor sign from her; the nearer she chose to come, the better for the *Richard*. The clocks below ticked on for another quarter of an hour before Jones heard a voice hailing across the two hundred yards of water, now silver-spangled by the risen moon.

"I cannot hear what you say," was the answer. Perhaps he did not hear; certainly the range was closing every moment.

"Answer at once or I shall fire," came clearly. At this a lad below in the *Richard* shouted "Fire and be damned!"

The Commodore must have bitten his lip with vexation at this bit of gallery shouting, for he had wished to show his enemies that they grossly maligned him when they called him a low bred pirate, and had intended to conduct the fight from the beginning with as much dignity as any captain in the Royal Navies of England or France.

However, it was time to begin. He gave the order to fire a second or two ahead of the British broadside. Meantime, the two frigates of the American squadron were closing round the *Countess of Scarborough*. For Captain Piercy there could have been little hope from the beginning. Obviously, with the two big ships closely engaged, he could not expect immediate assistance. Nevertheless he seems to have hoped on gallantly for nearly two hours before he struck to the *Pallas*. The *Alliance* is said to have sailed round and round the combatants, firing indiscriminately at both. It is a remarkable story. Captain Pierre Landais in the *Alliance* needs must have a paragraph or two to himself later on.

At the second broadside, two of the *Richard's* 18-pounders exploded, causing great material havoc and heavy casualties. It must have been terribly dishearten-

Flamborough Head

ing and increased an already considerable disparity in cannon between the principals, hastening Jones in his plan for an early boarding.

Seaman that he was, Paul Jones had good hold of his ship and handled her as well as any man could have handled her, but he was now up against a nimbler vessel handled by a man little less able, and an early attempt to board was quickly foiled. The *Serapis* was being maneuvered in such a way as to give more than she took in the way of punishment. Besides the material damage of clipping wings, it became necessary to attack personnel. Being well acquainted with the internal economy of a man-of-war he knew that Pearson would rely on the master and his mates for the actual handling of the ship; he knew the prime seamen were at the helm.

Heavy musketry fire was therefore concentrated on the wheel, standing exposed on the quarterdeck. Jones claimed afterwards to have shot down eleven men there, and although Pearson, we may be sure, was a good average seaman, it could not be expected of him that he was as good as the men whose principal duty was the handling of the ship to his orders. Jones here had an advantage over his opponent; he had been a sailing master most of his life. We may reckon, then, that as the action progressed the maneuvering qualities of the *Serapis* deteriorated and that the deterioration was not only due to loss of sail power. Nevertheless, Pearson avoided the contact which he feared for an hour and a quarter, during which time casualties were mounting in both ships and the *Richard's* sides were being splintered and driven in.

The wind, now westerly, was falling light, causing the smoke to hang like a pall over the ships. At 8:30 p.m., the *Richard*, which had been lying on the weather bow of the *Serapis*, was observed by Pearson to be falling broadside on top of him. He made an effort to swing the ship's head to port, so as to pass clear under his antagonist's stern but he was blanketed and had lost way; his jib-boom and the American's mizzen shrouds became entangled.

Jones sprang aft like a tiger and himself made all secure with a lashing.

Here I thought the dramatists had forgotten to put in a speech, but soon discovered in one account that he is reported as having said, "Now I have you!" Certain it is he had his man and from that moment it only became a matter of time.

Thus the two ships hung until the spar carried away, when, the tangle of rigging still holding, the two ships swung starboard to starboard side, head to stern, and the fluke of the *Serapis'* anchor at her bow hooked firmly into the quarter of the *Richard*. In this position they were to remain to the end in spite of Pearson's efforts to hack himself clear — all anticipated by the Americans and met with a withering fire of musketry. As a last hope the British ship let go an anchor from her disengaged side, thinking that, as the two swung to the northwesterly stream, the *Richard* would swing clear. She hung on.

Marksmen in the tops and from the higher sides of the ex-Indiaman fired down upon the exposed decks of the snugger-built 44-gun ship, helping to make her upper deck uninhabitable; her guns remained, while their crews lay dead or wounded beside them; that was on the upper deck. Below, in the 18-pounder battery there were few casualties, so that salvo after salvo went crashing through into the lower deck of the *Richard*, a deck from which Jones had long cleared his men. The damage at this period, therefore, was mainly material in the American ship, while in the *Serapis* the men were falling fast. On the upper deck the Americans were confident of victory, it was well within sight seemingly.

However, it is easy to understand the panic which ensued for a time when news spread amongst those above of the conditions below. They were indeed serious; for the ship was settling down with several feet of water in her hold. It was then that the Master-at-Arms on his own responsibility decided to release the British prisoners in hold. When Paul Jones saw these men tumbling up from below he met them with a sharp order, "Get to the pumps!" One man among the prisoners was as ready as Captain Jones, with a shout of, "Let the pumps alone and let the ruddy pirate sink." There was room for one man only in the *Richard* that night, the other was promptly shot. His name is unknown.

It would seem it was at this period that there were cries for quarter and firing ceased from the American ship, leading the British captain to hail if she had surrendered. A modern American writer summarizes the answers said to have been made. On the authority of Jones' own journal it was: "I have no intention of surrendering but am resolved to make you ask for quarter." Earlier he had told Benjamin Franklin that he had answered Pearson "in the most determined negative;" while on the authority of the French orderly Pierre Gerard the reply was, "No! I am just now beginning to fight," and it is this last, as all the world knows, the dramatists adopted.

Whatever may have been said, all was wasted on the person addressed. He declared he heard no answer to repeated hailing, and therefore ordered his people

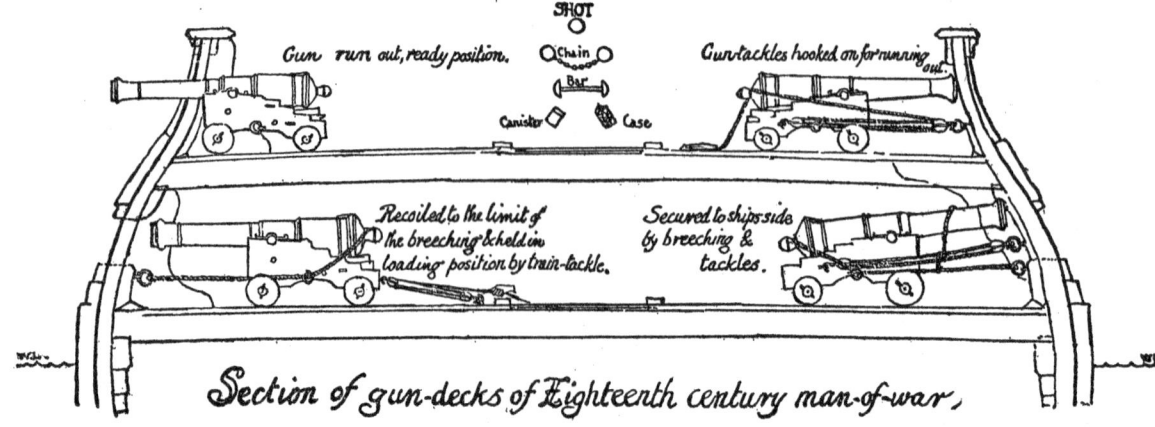

Section of gun-decks of Eighteenth century man-of-war.

to board. It was they who received the answer. Those who were not shot as they mounted the rail, by the remnant of the French marines, were stabbed or clubbed as they fell into the *Richard*, whose upper deck was full of men sheltering under the bulwarks. To Pearson it was obvious there could be no second attempt. There remained nothing else but to keep his heavy cannon thundering away. With the flash of the guns the sides of both ships were often on fire and clouds of black smoke rose and hung over the fight.

The *Alliance* appeared. Jones, hoping to indicate his own ship in this muddle of smoke, flame and flash, hoisted recognition light signals — apparently to no purpose. Jones was under the impression that he received the whole of his consort's broadside; Pearson took the broadside as meant for him, he received more than he wanted of it.

The position for some time appeared to be a stalemate. No doubt the survivors of the forty small arms men sheltering under the *Serapis'* forecastle continued to make good shooting when a target presented, but they were a small party, and one may suppose that Jones' difficulty in bringing his people to the point of boarding was due to the great variety in nationality and language amongst them. With conditions as they were below, however, something had to be done and done quickly.

The men in the *Richard's* tops had been well supplied with grenades and by their means the *Serapis* had been set on fire many times. Now Lieutenant Fanning and a seaman, laying out along the main yard which projected over the British ship, were enabled after one or two failures, to drop a grenade down the main hatch. This ignited the "ready" ammunition lying in the wake of the nearest gun and the flash shooting aft exploded the rest of the ready cartridges.

The effect was terrible. The battle lanterns were put out, and in the darkness and suffocating smoke the only light came from flickering rope's ends, burning splinters and the clothing of dead and maimed men.

An officer with flaming clothes was seen to jump overboard.

Lieutenant Stanhope climbed back later to rally his men, but only the guns forward of the main hatch were able to resume. It is reckoned that this single grenade was responsible for fifty-eight casualties.

(A too ready ammunition service was to bring to British arms a far more terrible disaster in 1916, when three great battle cruisers and one armored cruiser were utterly destroyed.)

The battle drew towards an end. In the early part Jones had aimed largely at his enemy's masts and rigging and there had never been at any time an opportunity to make damage good, so that the *Serapis'* mainmast had long been in a precarious condition. It is likely that fires outboard had scorched or burned the lanyards of the main shrouds, and it wanted but a light air or a gentle roll to bring all by the board. Somewhere about 10:30 p.m., one or the other occurred and the mast came crashing down. The *Alliance* reappeared about the time Jones called his boarders away. There was an abortive attempt at repulse from under the forecastle of the *Serapis*. Then Captain Pearson walked aft and hauled down the colors.

He turned to meet Lieutenant Richard Dale, First of the *Bon Homme Richard*, who requested him to pass over to the American ship, and there on her quarter-deck Captain Richard Pearson surrendered his sword to Captain John Paul Jones who, receiving it, expressed the hope that King George would grant a reward for a brave defense. The late Captain of His Majesty's Ship *Serapis* bowed slightly and with a tight lip passed below. It must have been a bitter moment for him, but as he looked about he realized he was on board a ship whose condition put her beyond power of causing mischief to the convoy; herein he found comfort.

The victors had little time for elation that night. Both ships were as bloody shambles. The *Richard* was only keeping afloat on her pumps; her prize, besides being short of a mainmast and mizzen topmast, was all cut to pieces aloft. The *Pallas* was largely preoccupied with her own capture, the *Countess of Scarborough*, while the *Alliance* seemed to think she had fulfilled her duty by sailing around. What had become of Captain Ricot in the *Vengeance* nobody seems to have worried to note. They were on an enemy coast and, although the patrols had been put on a false scent, by this time ships would be on their way round. Paul Jones was not proposing to wait for them.

The brilliancy with which he had fought the action hardly outshines the energy put forth to get all his squadron safe to port, but it soon became manifest that nothing could save the *Bon Homme Richard* and about ten the next morning she settled by the head and went down.

For a hundred and thirty-five years nothing disturbed her slumbers; then ship after ship came down to join her, and she now lies well within hail of many a merchantman whose steel frames are slowly dissolving and suffering a sea change. While she, with her oak timbers hardening, is likely to survive them all to sleep on alone.

The weather which had been so beautiful broke up, and the North Sea became itself again. On board the *Serapis* were the remnants of the two crews, many of whom were terribly wounded and burnt. The two surgeons did their best, but it was a losing game, many dying while the battered and jury-rigged ship was driven about in the autumn gales. By October 6th all had limped into the Texel, a neutral port; it was a case of "any port in a storm."

Paul Jones had fought a good fight and had every reason to expect that ascent of the ladder of fame from henceforth would be easier. It was not to be. At once he found himself enmeshed in the intricacies of International Law. Holland, being at the moment at peace with England, could not harbor a belligerent. Sir Joseph Yorke, the British Ambassador, denounced him as "the pirate John Paul of Scotland, a rebel subject and a criminal of the State." The Dutch thought the ambassador went too far. Whatever might be said of his past, the man carried himself with dignity and held a commission from Congress, so he was given ample time to refit before getting a notice to quit. The British Government was not his only trouble. Mixed with much adulation there was jealousy, and French sentiment was probably inclined to claim a larger share of glory for their own countrymen than the Americans were prepared to give, while the American faction attempted to belittle achievement. Taking everything together, Paul Jones began to feel he was only just beginning to fight.

Detraction to one of his temperament was hard to bear at any time; now, when newly confirmed in a belief in himself as the man ordained to found and command a great fleet under the American flag, anything and anybody standing in the way must be swept aside. Small wonder, therefore, that the shortcomings of consorts were emphasized, and that he did not go out of his way to check friends in the exaggeration of the force which had been opposed to him; in one so emotional and with such a burning ambition it was natural and, I think, forgivable. I am not so sure that it is natural — however forgivable — to take as absolute truth the statements made by men when the fever runs high in them.

It is a little difficult to separate what he said from what his friends thought he said or thought he ought to have said, but the sum total of it all (which now passes as truth in popular history) is that Captain Cottineau of the *Pallas* was timid or worse, Ricot of the *Vengeance* was no better, while Landais of the *Alliance* has had a bucket full of epithets capsized over his head, besides being accused of a definite act of treachery on the night of September 23rd. It is also hinted that the French marines, who formed more than a third of the crew of the *Richard*, were not as steady as they might have been. There does not seem much left to praise, but the popular stories are generous to those Americans who fought immediately around him.

Evidently Pierre Landais was nobody's darling. For an opening, he is described as a discredited and disreputable French officer who first came to the United States in charge of a convoy of stores for Rochambeau's army. The General could have been none too pleased when he heard that a man of no credit had been placed in charge of his supplies, for even in those days it was known that an army fights on its belly. Disrepute and all, Landais was made a citizen of the United States and given command of a beautiful new American frigate, shortly afterwards coming into Paul Jones' life to pester him.

One gathers that the squadron's first attempt to launch the attack on British commerce was brought to nought by Landais' misconduct. Two days after leaving L'Orient, the *Alliance* and the *Richard* were in violent collision, due it was said to the former's disobeying signals, and it was suspected that the misfortune was in some way connected with a plot amongst British prisoners to seize the *Richard*. However, the subsequent court martial, held when the damaged ships returned to harbor, suspended the sailing master of the *Richard* and ordered two quartermasters to be flogged.

Very soon after the final departure, the best privateersman parted company because he could not abide Landais, describing him as no gentleman. Then one day off the Irish Coast Landais appeared over the rail of the *Richard*, his face distorted with rage, blaming and abusing Jones for the loss of two of the ship's boats and their crews. Boats and men belonged to the *Richard;* surely the "Concordat" left Paul Jones in command of his own ship, if it did not give him control over Master Landais? On the face of it, the man was either mutinous or mad. However, no steps were taken either by captain or doctor to supersede him and he was left to pursue unchecked his evil ways.

Refusing to confer with his fellow captains and, as we know, taking French leave of the squadron as it suited him, near Cape Wrath, where two prizes valued at £40,000 were captured, Landais on his own responsibility sent them into a Danish port and neutral Denmark was persuaded to return the ships to England. The American squadron saw £40,000 going west; small wonder that Master Pierre was generally unpopular with his fellows.

Despite the fact that all hands describe him as endeavoring to keep out of Jones' way, Landais did, as we have seen, turn up at the rendezvous on the 23rd of September. In the opening moves he is said to have disobeyed the signal to form the line, even making as though he would go for the convoy, he being described as out for plunder only. This last is demonstrably untrue, for as soon as his consorts had engaged the two British ships there was nothing to stop him from making straight for the convoy, a fleet insured for £600,000 sterling. He did not do so. But although he remained on the field of battle, American accounts with few exceptions insist that his presence had no effect on the action against the British. Indeed they go further and maintain that he assisted the enemy, when by accident or design he fired into both the *Richard* and the *Pallas*, at that time hotly engaged.

Although modern British authors generally demur at the suggestion that the presence of the *Alliance* had no effect on the action, they seem inclined to accept the worst urged against Landais and to ignore entirely the evidence of Captain Pearson. Perhaps they have in mind earlier English treatment of the story of Paul Jones and are a little ashamed and wish to make amends, or perhaps they refrain from putting the other side of the story merely out of what they imagine to be politeness — a poor compliment to pay to Americans in supposing they are not prepared to stand to a plain argument or respect anyone the less for standing up for his own side.

There is an old story about a seaman who was being flogged. The captain, who stood by, found fault with the way the executioner was handling the cat o' nine tails, considering he was not laying on with sufficient strength. Hearing the remonstrance, the poor fellow being flogged turned his head and addressing his captain with what we may imagine some feeling, said, "All I ask for is the fair thing. This here man is adoing of his duty properly, and I reckon I ought to know!" So I think Captain Pearson might be permitted to say a word as to whether the *Alliance* had any effect in bringing about his discomfiture. It was he who was being beaten and, although his evidence might be prejudiced, it cannot be described as entirely irrelevant. He at any rate reckoned he ought to know and this is what he said:

"At the same time the largest of the two frigates kept sailing around us the whole action, raking us fore and aft, by which means she killed or wounded almost every man on the quarter and main decks." And, later in this despatch, which was dated October 6th from on board the *Pallas* while he was prisoner, he goes on to say: "The frigate coming across our stern and pouring her broadside into us again without our being able to bring a gun to bear on her I found it in vain . . . to stand out any longer with the least prospect of success. I therefore struck."

Captain Piercy of the *Scarborough* was likewise under the impression that in the early part of the action he was engaged first by one frigate and later by another. But it will be said that this evidence is clean contrary to the evidence of Paul Jones who declares that the *Alliance* fired her broadsides into the *Richard*.

The answer is that Jones in the heat of the action was no more aware than Pearson what share the other ship had of Landais' broadsides. It is conceivable that the Indiaman, looming much larger than the man-of-war, received the "overs" intended for the *Serapis*. All that Jones was aware of was that his men were being hit, and we can quite understand his fury.

That the excitable Landais did fire a broadside into the *Richard*, even though she hoisted lights, is not improbable. Three oil lamps hoisted in a miniature reproduction of the infernal regions would make a poor showing. With both ships closely interlocked, both on fire in several places, and both more often than not thickly enshrouded, with moonlight distorting rather than defining all, who could tell where the lights were hoisted, when fitfully they became visible? Those with even a very slight experience of night operations in sea warfare know well enough the mishaps that may, nay, have happened in modern times under similar conditions. But there is no need to bring forward their evidence when there is the evidence of an eyewitness of how things appeared on this particular night of war fog in 1779.

Captain Thomas Piercy of the *Scarborough*, in his report to his senior officer dated October 6th, says that after one of the frigates had left him, "I made sail up to the *Serapis* to see if I could give you any assistance, but on coming near you I found you and the enemy so close together and covered with smoke that I could not distinguish one ship from another, and for fear I might fire into the *Serapis* instead of the enemy I backed the main topsail in order to engage the attention of one of the frigates that was then coming up."

Now this evidence was not concocted with a view to absolve Landais of a charge of treachery, for Piercy could have had no interest in Landais. It stands as an independent statement. It may be used as evidence that the *Alliance* acted recklessly by firing at all, or it may be used as a defense when her captain is accused of failing to render adequate assistance, and it can be used as an explanation of why a man with an ill-balanced mind entirely lost control of himself when accused of deliberately firing upon his friends.

Efforts were made at his trial and a great deal of trouble has been taken since to bring the charge of treachery home to this wretched man. It has been said that the damage to the port side of the *Richard* was the principal cause of her sinking; diagrams have been drawn showing definitely (as is the way of diagrams) that the *Serapis* was not at any time in a position to inflict this damage. Therefore, we are to understand the American ship went down, not, as had been supposed, as the result of British gunnery, but by the villainous treachery of Pierre Landais.

That these diagrams are constructed on the testimony of eyewitnesses will be for many conclusive; they will convict the Captain of the *Alliance*. On the other hand, those who have listened to a collision case in an admiralty court, or even a protest case in a yacht race, will not be so easily convinced. They will know how strong is "the will to believe" manifested by witnesses generally. In this particular case — one of the fiercest naval actions on record, and a night action at that — they will wonder how people could be so definite where a few yards or a momentary alteration of course by a couple of points of the compass would, I suppose, have made the difference. It is illuminating, though not surprising, to read that the first lieutenant of the *Richard* was unaware until after the surrender that the second phase of the action had been fought at anchor.

It is not good to swear positively to time, direction, or the sequence of events after violent action; it is better to testify only to the best of one's belief. Perhaps the definite nature of the evidence of some of the witnesses against Landais shook the belief of Congress in their testimony. That he did the fatal damage to the *Richard*; that he was mad, may have been accepted, but that he acted treacherously could not have been believed, for you do not let a criminal lunatic go free; you do not grant a life pension to a traitor.

That Captain Pearson exaggerated the effect of the *Alliance's* action against himself is I think possible; he was on his defense and was of the sons of Adam. But according to some later, though pre-war British writers, even if he were correct in his valuation he is not absolved of blame for the loss of his ship for, they say, the *Serapis* was a match for the two ships together and she should have beaten them. Had Pearson known the precise details of the force against him, and knowing them had the choice of range, he would have agreed with his critics. He had no choice of range; he was deceived as to the force with which he was about to engage.

Not by the flicker of an eyelid would he have revealed to a soul what was passing in his mind, but we can hardly doubt that the captain of the *Serapis* went into action that night with the hope and determination of saving his convoy, and with little hope or expectation of saving himself or his consort. There is evidence of his having been under the impression that the largest of the three ships approaching was a 50-gun ship, that is to say, a vessel mounting 24-pounders as opposed to his 18-pounders. The *Alliance* would have appeared as an ordinary 32-gun frigate and the *Pallas* one of 28 guns. He could not by any means have known of the Commodore's domestic troubles with his subordinates and therefore even his most severe critics will admit that, according to his lights, he was about to engage a superior force — superior under any conditions.

In his despatch he states that the squadron approached end on and he was unable to distinguish their colors; we may suppose that it being an hour after sunset before they closed, he would not be much the wiser as to details of armament until he was in action. Although a short time before this he is said to have speculated as to whether he were not about to engage Paul Jones, there came no enlightenment in answer to a hail. According to him the answer was *"Princess Royal"*; after that, mere evasion and then the guns.

Perhaps he should have taken the chance of the squadron's being hostile and opened fire sooner than he did; perhaps he should have realized he was being enticed nearer to his disadvantage, but it is doubtful whether either made much difference. The thicker the atmosphere grew, the more anxious the man with the convoy on his mind would be to keep near his enemy, and in deceptive light and much smoke the man determined to fall on board is pretty sure of succeeding in the end — I should think so, but I do not know.

Paul Jones may have smiled at Pearson's formal challenge before battle, but his bright mind would have appreciated to the full his opponent's difficulties. He foresaw them and they were the margin whereby he reckoned to win.

The concentration of his fire on the hull of the *Richard*, and the neglect to attempt to cripple by knocking away her spars, is criticism seeming to have more substance in it. To have winged her so that she was unable to pursue the convoy, seems to have been the obvious procedure for the British captain. But here again he was no doubt governed by his first conception of the situation, and perhaps he was not so very far out in his reluctance to change from the technique of battle to which he had been bred.

Naval gunnery was not a very exact science in the eighteenth century; the number of hits registered on such comparatively small targets as masts and spars would not be very great, and here a miss was as good as a mile; whereas a shot aimed low at the hull generally found a billet. The French practice of firing on the upward roll of the ship naturally helped their winging policy, while the British way of firing on the downward roll assisted the policy which was theirs — the spoiling of the aim of the marksmen and manslaughter.

Obviously in faded light even good marksmen make the poorer shooting. Pearson knew he could not afford to throw away a shot, and he hoped that by hammering and hammering away at the hull of the *Richard* he would leave her in no heart to attack the fleet of forty merchantmen, the protection of which in the words of his instructions was "his most particular duty."

And for the rest I believe Richard Pearson did not so greatly care. "I am extremely sorry," he wrote, "for the misfortune that has happened, that of losing His Majesty's ship I had the honour to command; but at the same time I flatter myself with the hopes that their Lordships will be convinced that she has not been given away; but, on the contrary, that every exertion has been used to defend her, and that two essential pieces of service to our country have arisen from it; the one in wholly oversetting the cruise and intentions of this flying squadron; the other in rescuing the whole of a valuable convoy from falling into the hands of the enemy, which must have been the case had I acted any otherwise than I did."

Paul Jones' indignant denial of having said on hearing of the knighthood bestowed on the Captain of the *Serapis* that he would help him to an earldoom at their next meeting, is now perhaps understandable. For a wit to have said it was well enough — for wits win battles with their mouths — but it would have been unpardonable in one who had fought through that desperate struggle in the dark when, in the two ships, nearly four hundred men had been killed or wounded. The bouquets and the garlands, the honeyed praise and flattery might intoxicate him at his first coming home from sea, as they have intoxicated many a man with less excuse, but the memory of that moonlit bloody battle had made far too deep an impression to be coupled with a jest.

He remembered the approach and the early disaster in the *Richard's* lower deck battery calling for great fortitude to surmount; he remembered the long hour when his ship was being shot from under him; he remembered when close contact was made with the hope of early victory, how it had been checked by the resistance of a smaller disciplined crew holding his larger mixed crowd. Burned deep into memory was that sudden panic when his people called for quarter, when there came the eruption of a hundred of his prisoners from below — that had been a terrible moment — when all his foresight seemed about to be flung away and all his valor wasted. He had met all but it had drawn from him the last reserves of heart and mind. Aye, he knew there had been earned honor enough and to spare for both the Chevalier John Paul Jones and Sir Richard Pearson on the night of September 23rd, 1779.

The fame of Paul Jones as a fighting seaman rests in the main on the battle off Flamborough Head. It was there he was able to appraise the theories of naval warfare to be learned from books. The lessons were clear and unmistakable.

There would be no hunting for personal glory and there would be no use in many ships unless they fought as a unit. There would not be time for the old pomp and formality of war and many old conventions would need to be knocked away; nevertheless there would be no room for democratic rule.

Strange to say, the "New Model" for a navy, taking shape in his mind, resembled very little his own victorious squadron, with its too easy discipline and license in thought and action. He would have realized that many of his conclusions would be unacceptable in a country in the first flush of a new freedom and of a sturdy individualism. He was right in his reckoning, for on his return his ideas made little progress in America, and finally when peace came with independence he was to learn sadly how true was the saying of a wise old statesman that "soldiers in peace time are as chimney-pots in summer."

A man without a home, the only road open to him was that of a soldier of fortune and he took it, and Fortune, as is her way, soon turned her face from him. Yet surely as he lay dying, alone and neglected in a strange land, he foresaw that the nation for which as a young man he had drawn his sword would one day come to remember the name of John Paul Jones and the navy he had dreamt of would come into being.

INDEX

INDEX

CPSIA information can be obtained
at www.ICGtesting.com
Printed in the USA
BVHW010913260421
605871BV00003B/456